International Business Control, Reporting and Corporate Governance

Georges Nurdin

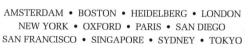

AMSTERDAM • BOSTON • HEIDELBERG • LONDON
NEW YORK • OXFORD • PARIS • SAN DIEGO
SAN FRANCISCO • SINGAPORE • SYDNEY • TOKYO

CIMA Publishing is an imprint of Elsevier

CIMA Publishing is an imprint of Elsevier
Linacre House, Jordan Hill, Oxford OX2 8DP, UK
30 Corporate Drive, Suite 400, Burlington, MA 01803, USA

British Library Cataloguing in Publication Data
A catalogue record for this book is available from the British Library

ISBN: 978-0-7506-8383-8

For information on all CIMA publishing publications
visit our web site at books.elsevier.com

Typeset by Charon Tec Ltd., A Macmillan Company. (www.macmillansolutions.com)

Printed and bound in Great Britain

09 10 11   10 9 8 7 6 5 4 3 2 1

Table of contents

List of figures

Foreword

The controller's challenge

At last! A book on *International Business Controlling* not centred on basic detailed descriptions of techniques to be used to exercise this function. Georges Nurdin very rightly puts the focus on the indispensable recognition of the impact of cultural differences of all type, which condition the success of businesses and of course the effectiveness of the controllership function.

So few, of those who are supposed to prepare the future generations of controllers, transmit these essential major messages in their courses and in their writings. All companies are not alike either by the nature of their activities, products, geographical location, style of management, nationality, etc. Every chapter herein stresses again and again the fundamental need for the controller to recognise that all business cannot be monitored the same way.

What is underlined and results from George Nurdin's descriptions of "differences" for the controller' function is that he is not to be confused with an accountant, be it a cost accountant. He is not in charge of production of reports and statistics. His function cannot be restricted to be an analyst of the past performances of his company.

His fundamental mission is to assist the managers, at whatever level, to take appropriate decisions which will guarantee the attainment and maintainability of strategic objectives, throughout their business, in face of continual evolution of the environment, markets, products and competition. His key task is to help the managers to anticipate the long-range perspectives and related alternatives of the changing world conditions as they will affect the economics of his company.

To achieve this mission implies that the controller, at whatever level he is positioned in the company organisation, fully understands what his company is all about. Even though he may be the controller of a unit far away from headquarters or of a functional activity in a remote area and at a secondary hierarchic level, he imperatively must have gotten familiarised with the company's environment, products, activities, etc. (And, of course, as "controller", he cannot exercise his function without an adequate knowledge of the company's accounting and information systems, which are some of his everyday tools.)

I also consider very important not only for his knowledge of the activities, but also to acquire credibility towards the operating line managers that, he must have had a "hands-on" training on the activities of the company (unit, plant, sales office, subsidiary, etc.), to which he is assigned. In the course of this familiarisation programme, he needs to be briefed on its key success and risk factors.

By "hands on", I wish to stress that this is not as a casual "observer", who looks over the shoulders of the person doing the job, but as a "doer". This means that if the company or unit is focalised towards production, to effectively "work" for a short period of time on the production line. The same apply if it is a sales subsidiary where he should be a "salesman" for a couple of weeks. These moments of actually "touching the roots" of his business will be the best preparation for him for his future tasks. He will have "touched" the day-to-day activities and also he will have a concrete sense of the human relations existing therein.

It is of course also basic that the controller understands what is, and what should be, his role. From a "number pusher" to producing financial reports, ... from an analyst of the past looking at the business in a "rear view mirror" to a professional obsessed by what will be the results of tomorrow, ... from being the expert in profitability analysis to a financial spokesman, ... and most fundamental and essential ... a team pilot associating all actors in the search for improvement of the future financial performances of the operations.

The key words for the controller are: objectives, key success targets, opportunities and risks assumptions, strategy, scenario, validation, traceability, follow-up, performance analysis, promote reactivity, action plans ... and always ... *communication*!

The most frequent reasons for the failure of the controller are his inadequate adjustment and phasing to the culture of his company and its environment. His technical competence is useless without his ability to understand the cultural environment and the continual changes in the "outside world" which his company has to face. Having acquired this knowledge, if he is not able to listen, communicate, explain and convince, he will never be considered as part of the "team".

The controller will have to face many challenges in his professional life: "resistance to change", egocentrique motivations, feudality of management, fear by the operating managers to lose their prestige, lack of confidence: "we have already tried this solution ...", useless complexity, lack of adequate competence in the operating line, and last but not least, credibility weakness of the controller function ...

In face of these negative factors, the controller must be able to show his ability to effectively contribute to the management by bringing an objective financial "present and *future* vision" and thanks to this, be a competent "navigator" capable to assist the men at the helm to attain *THEIR objectives.*

This will require:

- technical competence;
- ability to move in a world of uncertainty;
- objectivity under all circumstances;
- to be a "simplificator" thru his communication;
- to be a "self-starter", always in search for factors which will improve profitability;
- to play a dynamic and proactive role without substituting himself to the operating line;
- to keep cool and control his emotions;
- and overall to *have economic business sense*;
- *and last, but not the least important, be courageous!*

These abilities are not given to everyone!

It's the responsibility of those professionals in charge of the selection and training of the future generation of controllers such as university teachers, personnel consultants, recruitment firms, etc. to be fully familiar of these major characteristics of the function. Too many young students, or junior professionals, are mislead and thereafter ambition, or accept to take on, a function for which they are fundamentally not made for.

It is also essential that the controller, in his career development, recognises and accepts his own "limits". Throughout my years as Chief

Financial Officer in various companies and countries I have seen, on and on again, failures in the performance of what were believed to be seasoned controllers. These were essentially due to errors in judgement by the hierarchy or the consequence of non-adapted ambitions of the controller himself.

All men, whatever their competence, are not made for all environments …

- Send a brilliant controller, extremely thorough in his time-consuming reviews, in a country where inflation is exploding … and you have a disaster! Before he has prepared his presentation to management his subsidiary may have lost millions!
- Ask a sharp controller to expose himself in a presentation to the manufacturing staff, without knowing the language of the factory foremen and you can be sure that his excellent analysis is good for the waste paper basket!
- Transfer an excellent controller from a manufacturing unit to a sales subsidiary, one can be assured that it will take time for him to adjust to the "approximate evaluation" methods to determine and explain variances of performances and forecast assumptions!
- Transfer a "Latin" controller of a large company to the headquarter of an American major, and he will be put in "purgatory" by his American colleagues!
- Observe the bewilderment of a seasoned controller, who has resigned from his long-standing and established company, to join a start-up, hoping thereby to have more recognition and prestige, battling to be "heard" when stressing the importance of respecting performance ratios!
- Even though having had an excellent record as a "business" controller become a controller of a company centred on R&D and you can be assured that you will be put in "limbo"!
- And finally, but of course not being exhaustive in these examples, satisfy your ambitions, and go from a state owned business to a private entrepreneurial company (the same is of course true the other way), and you can bet that the "suffering" will be hard to overcome!

We can go on and on, taking every one of the chapters of this excellent book, to illustrate that all men are not all made for each and every condition described by Georges Nurdin!

Unless, of course, that they attentively read this book and compare their personalities, competences, etc. with the prerequisites implied by the varying situations in this changing world.

Stephan Doblin

Ex Chief Financial Officer of 3M France and Italy, Roussel-Uclaf, WR. Grace Europe, Bendix Europe, Fiat Automobile and Vice-President Planning and Control of Renault.

Co-founder of the French Financial Executives Association.

About the author

Georges Nurdin was born and grew up in the Pacific Region where during his formative years he was soon exposed to the immense variety and richness of ethnological, national and regional cultures, as well as to the biodiversity which has no equivalent in the world, ranging from New Caledonia, Fiji, Tahiti, Vanuatu, Australia, Wallis and Futuna, Indonesia, to New Zealand.

On reaching Europe after completing the equivalent of four Bachelors in Mathematics, History, Economics and Philosophy with distinction he was admitted to the French "elite higher education schools" called the "Grandes Ecoles". He graduated from the European School of Management ESCP-EAP where he completed a pan-European Master of Science in Management which enabled him to study business, economics and management in Paris (France), Oxford (UK) and Berlin (Germany) which he later complemented with an American MBA programme.

Georges is a Doctoral Fellow (PhD) of the Conservatoire National des Arts et Metiers (French equivalent to MIT) in International Economics and Trade. At the same time Georges also studied and practiced Budo (traditional Japanese martial Arts).

For the past 20 years Georges has held several International Senior Executive positions (inter alia Global Divisional CEO and European CFO) in leading American MNCs, including Du Pont de Nemours and General Electric as well as in European MNCs with Landis & Gyr/ Siemens, Ascom and Valéo.

Over the last 10 years Georges has been advising the senior management of International Private and Public sector companies, Governmental Agencies, NGOs and International Organisations including the United Nations and the World Health Organization, focusing on international and cross-cultural management.

Georges also regularly lectures in European universities and business schools in Executive Education and MBA programmes, and has authored many articles and given conferences throughout the world.

Georges is the founding chairman of the Global Institute for *Eco*-development and *Cross-Cultural Management* – the EC^2M Institute, and is a Fellow of the Institute of Directors, London, as well as a Fellow of the DFCG, the French Institute of Financial Executives.

His senior executive and director roles, consulting assignments, lectures, publications and conferences span across many sectors such as Energy, Petrochemicals, Automotive, Cosmetics, Electronics, Education, Extractive Industries, Construction and Engineering, Security systems, Aeronautics, Health, Pharmaceuticals, Leisure and Tourism, Transports, Communications, and United Nation agencies.

His experience spans across countries and regions where he has lived or worked including: South Africa, Northern Africa, Argentina, Australia, Austria, the Baltic Republics, Brazil, China, the Czech Republic, France, Germany, Hungary, Near East and Middle East, Poland, Russia, Slovak Republic, Romania, Spain, Sweden, Switzerland, UK and USA.

Georges speaks English, French, German and Spanish, and has a good command of Bishlamar (Vanuatu, Oceania) and a working knowledge of Drehu (Melanesian dialect), reads and writes Latin and Ancient Greek and has passion for History and the Arts.

georges.nurdin@ec2m.org

Preface

Globalisation is at work today more than yesterday, and even more than what it will be tomorrow. One would be considered either deaf or a hermit to not have heard it been said repeatedly for the past years. Bob Dylan did not say anything different in 1966: "times they are a changing".

Thus, if everything has already been said then why another book on controlling, monitoring and managing in a global context.

In other words, *if the world was really going global*, it would pose lesser problems to management, because finally the phase that the world is flat (Friedman, 2005) has arrived, which would then leave only two dimensions to monitor; things would definitely become simpler, then why bother?

However, exactly the opposite is happening in the real world. The world is getting more and more complex.

Firstly, the *world is not going global*, not even globalising; the world *is global* by its very nature, since 4.5 billions years. It was created spherical (globus in Latin). However, the world is full of diversity and the human norm of uniformity is an alien concept.

Secondly, the *inter-nations* business is drastically increasing in terms of trading goods and services, Foreign Direct Investment (FDI), outsourcing design, off shoring manufacturing, establishing trans-continental Just in Time, supply chain, intellectual property (technology, licensees, franchises, music, movies, literature, etc.); thus cultural interfaces and interactions are increasing exponentially, creating either major potential clashes (Huntington, 1996) or major potential opportunities on which to leverage – all depending on *how and whether cultural interfacing is managed in the course of doing international business.*

Thirdly, the "world" government is shifting away from sovereign states and moving into the hands of multinational corporations (MNCs) at a magnitude and pace it has never occurred. Among the top 20 world economies, more than half are MNCs, who are already spreading their corporate culture, power and influence across nations, literally shaping the world in which we live, competing with and sometimes challenging, or confronting millennia-long societies and their national cultural values.

Fourthly, corporations are ultimately controlled by institutional funds (66% of New York–listed stocks are in the hands of 100 funds today, whereas it was just 1% in 1960) which are, by nature, share "flippers", not share "holders" anymore. They, inter alia, spur the international M&A's tidal wave which after the speculative climax have, in most cases, a failure rate of 75%.

Lastly, and more importantly, the world ecosystem is on the verge of bankruptcy; be it in terms of freshwater resources, oil depletion, air and water, soil and electromagnetic pollution, climate change or global warming.

This book, based on more than 30 years of extensive international experience at top-level management and 4 years of extensive research, addresses these challenges in a highly innovative way.

It provides a road map of how to effectively and efficiently control and monitor business that span across nations and cultures, and ways to increase and maintain performance, over a long period of time, which is sustainable and is in harmony with the environment.

It also helps in assessing and forecasting, via the I^2Q – the *I*nternational $\times$ *I*ntercultural *Q*uotient – the capacity to enjoy an enduring yet efficient international performance. This is a major breakthrough in the field of controlling since it provides answers beyond the P&L and cash flow statements and balance sheet to the key root performance drivers. It provides solutions that serve as a remedy and improve the root cause of the problems that could eventually result in very high rates of failure in international business, such as causing 75% of the international M&A failures.

The innovative concept, approach and tool outlined in this book do not have, to date, any equivalent in terms of depth and relevance.

The book also discusses about adopting innovative ways to practically control business and monitor function, as well as control environment and eco-efficiency levers which the business and industry need to handle urgently. The methods proposed are built on extensive research work developed at the Global Institute for *E*co-development and *C*ross *C*ultural *M*anagement – the EC^{2}M Institute – which provides new energy and light to this 21st century challenge.

To illustrate the concepts, the book taps into many real-life experiences, which have been adequately presented as "mini cases".

If you are someone who is at a business school, an accountant, controller, CFO or an executive as a CEO, business development manager, an investment banker, and are willing to learn about innovative ways to increase international performance in addressing issues that you are confronted within an international role, then this book is for you.

Georges Nurdin, BA, MSc, MBA, PhD, FinstD

georges.nurdin@ec2m.org

References

Friedman, T. (2005), *The World Is Flat, a Brief History of the 21st Century*.
Huntington, S. (1996), *The Clash of Civilization and the Remaking of the World Order*.

2

From domestic business controlling to international business controlling

2.1 From audit/procedures-based conformity to (co) piloting

The first forms of controlling date back to the Mesopotamian age, about 5500 years ago. It is striking to learn that the first thing man carried out after the invention of the writing was to actually perform controlling. In fact the early writings of ancient times are not philosophical or religious texts or artwork, but they are actually about livestock possession.

Even more amazing is that these were logged by writing with a stylus on clay, as some (elementary) sort of perpetual inventory (adding a bar when a new sheep was born, crossing out a bar when sold/dead). The ultimate purpose of this perpetual recording was a basic form of accounting enabling instant status of their assets (headcount of livestock) and auditing (checks) the current situation to identify any deviations (robbery, etc.).

The role of controlling has evolved to become more or less entangled with the role of auditing. In other words, controlling was "only" seen as auditing, and auditing was seen merely as spotting non-compliances or frauds.

It was only in the second part of the 19th century, in the wake of the Industrial Revolution, that auditing branched out into a distinctive role of external auditing, firstly in the United Kingdom, then in the United States (although with some difference in scope). This was a major breakthrough because till then the role of external auditors was limited to checking on management compliance and probity (absence of fraud or malpractice) and reporting to the firm's owners.

In the wake of 1929, world stock exchange collapsed and the law in the United States enforced that all listed companies' financial statements be "audited" by independent professionals; thus making the latter's reports a "fair and true view" of the company's actual financial situation.

As a result the CPA (Certified Public Accountant) was established as a professional body entitled to perform external audits and to subsequently certify any companies' accounts.

Note that the external auditors mostly rely on the compliance of strong internal company controls to perform their duties.

At the same time, "controlling" took up a distinctive role of its own that was geared towards the "piloting" of the corporation.

In 1917, Henri Fayol, a French manager, gave the very first impetus to this new dimension. He was a qualified engineer from the "elite" French school La Grande École (Ecole des Mines). Henri Fayol was a seasoned manager and after several top management positions he was appointed CEO of a large mining corporation.

In his famous book, published firstly in French in 1917 entitled *Administration Générale et Industrielle* and then in English in 1949 as *General and Industrial Administration*, Fayol theorised from his experience that management is composed of five fundamental functions:

(1) Planning
(2) Organising
(3) Commanding
(4) Coordinating
(5) Controlling.

From this point onwards, controlling was seen as a full-fledged management function and not "just" as an auditing tool aimed at identifying frauds or malpractices as was seen to be the case most of the time if not all the time in those days.

In the United Kingdom during the same period, the "Institute of Cost and Works Accountants" – now the CIMA (Chartered Institute of Management Accountants) – initially aimed at specialising in techniques for controlling manufacturing, services and the public sectors.

Similar to Henri Fayol, who considered controlling as a managerial function, although different in its approach (CIMA focuses on core business economics whereas Fayol focused on general management and corporate governance), the CIMA greatly contributed to adopt and make an operational distinction between audit and controlling (Fayol, 1917).

This was the dawn of an era where controlling became increasingly important, if not pivotal to business piloting. It was during this period that business started moving away from what used to be a single-product business, during the Industrial Revolution, to multiproducts/multidivisions/multisided international corporations – developing into an even greater complexity. In this context, "piloting" the business directly implied towards getting a grip over the core ever-complex, business economics and, inter alia, the cost accounting and management accountants.

Thus, controlling can be seen as a corporation co-pilot, e.g., a plane cockpit where both the captain (the chief executive officer (CEO)) and the controller (the co-pilot) navigate the aircraft.

Moving away from this historical perspective to a more recent development, the Sarbanes–Oxley Act (2002) passed in the United States enforces that financial accounts of all US-listed companies must be certified by both the CEO and the chief financial officer (CFO) in his/her controlling role, thus formalising the co-pilot's role in controlling the corporate management.

2.2   From "ex post" control to "ex ante" control

One of the major changes that occurred during the evolution of the controlling function is the capacity it developed towards the "future thinking" in the first part of the 20th century.

As controlling disentangled from auditing and the strict checking of non-compliance, fraud and malpractice moved towards a full-fledged general management function, controlling also embraced a new challenge: not only to look back at past events called the ex post (literally in Latin from behind; a typical audit inherited approach) but to look forward to the future (thus literally in Latin ex ante meaning from before) to manage better.

In concrete terms this approach has led controlling to develop a corpus of tools supporting the forward-looking attitude as a start in the form of plans and budgets. Not only this but the controlling scope also expanded to include investment appraisal techniques since investments are by essence future-oriented (future benefits/profits are meant to generate return many times the initial investment including a risk element).

The latter point is worth mentioning for being a major breakthrough as it was not the academia, but a corporation, who first recognised the importance of "scientifically" measuring the attractiveness of an investment rather than by virtue of its qualitative factors based on anticipated returns.

At beginning of the 20th century, Du Pont de Nemours called this method the "return on investment" (better known as ROI). Although they were amongst the world leaders in chemistry innovation and production, Du Pont recognised that it was equally important to invest in R&D in the controlling science (again the co-piloting concept shapes up) to be the world leader in economic- and financial performance. In brief, Du Pont related the future returns as expressed in profit & loss (P&L) incomes to the initial investment in the form of a ratio. For convenience, the return was expressed as an averaged profit, supposedly, representing a "standard profit" and the investment as the "gross" initial investment.

Naturally this method had many biases, all having been debated since then; but it had two major positive impacts that were real breakthroughs in the controlling field.

Firstly, the ROI was a tool that allowed investments to be "scientifically" and quantitatively appraised and more importantly compared throughout departments, divisions, business, corporations and counties. Investments could then be ranked and the access to internal and external funding be based on rational factors.

Secondly, and perhaps more fundamentally, the ROI was a "fractal concept". The fractals were mathematically characterised by Mandelbrot, a French mathematician, who coined the term in 1975 (fractals are structures which have the same properties/shapes, whatever the dimension; in other words, which unfold into a series of sub-ROI's cascading like Russian dolls).

The nominator, or the return, can be sub-specified in all its constituents: sales (by departments, products, countries, channels, etc.) and costs (into cost of manufacture, cost of marketing, cost of distribution, etc.). The same applies to the denominator (the investment) that can be split into working capital which can be further split into inventories, receivables, etc.

Allowing the ROI to be split into constituents helps to control and monitor the different management functions responsible for delivering these constituents, e.g., the sales department, the plant operations, the logistics department and credit controlling.

Controlling also adopted planning and budgeting as part of the "ex ante" forward-looking approach.

Until the first oil crisis in 1973, the strategic planning horizon was pre-dicted for 10–20 years ahead based on the 30 years post-WWII; it was thought that a similar pattern of steady continuous growth would con-tinue to unfold forever.

Even the budget horizon was 12–24 months, where the first 12 months were a mere replica of the strategic plan.

2.3 From simple, linear and predictable to complex, turbulent, non-linear and non-predictable

The period after the 1973 oil crisis that extended up to the mid-seventies is seen in many ways as the turning point in controlling history.

It became clear that the steady ever-continuous growth was no longer the ruling paradigm and that the environment could have extreme fluctuations.

This had major consequences in controlling, and controllers soon began to develop tools that would help management in facing these new challenges.

The scenario method was introduced into the planning activities, not to be bound to a single anticipated pattern but to articulate and evaluate mul-tiple future possibilities; and consequently appraise their consequences. This has given rise to the famous "what if" approach to controlling.

Whilst planning, the sensitivities analyses were introduced to gauge the sensitivity of expected results to the possible fluctuations in several fac-tors or operating conditions (energy prices fluctuations, demand fluctu-ations, price fluctuations, etc.).

Budgeting activities were also revamped or adapted to face this paradigm change.

Flex budgets were introduced along with rolling forecasts, allowing a degree of linkage to be introduced between the fluctuations of rev-enues and the relative adjustments of costs; protecting a certain level of profitability through some kind of quasi-instant response mechanism to fluctuations in revenues or costs proved to be a very helpful contribu-tion by the controller to management and corporate owners.

US corporations also reacted by adopting the zero based budgeting (ZBB), theorised and operationalised, in the mid-seventies, by Peter Pyhrr, the controller of Texas Instrument.

The ZBB was opposed to the traditional incremental budgeting techniques that had been ruling for the past century. In essence, ZBB was revolutionary because it imposed a start from scratch approach for every budget cycle and took a fresh and challenging view into the future and thus created budgets in direct relationship to the business needs (up or down).

Downsizing was a "brutal" response towards cutting costs – cost being a result of fluctuating revenues and stagflation in the 1980s and re-engineering (the term was coined by Hammer and Champy (1993)) – an intelligent approach to overcome complexity where the controlling tools contributed towards making the controlling function evolve and meet the challenges of the troubled, non-linear economy.

In parallel with the turbulences imposed on the business world by huge variations in energy prices, inflation, currency fluctuations (the US dollar and all other currencies were in a state of turmoil following the 1973 relinquishment of the Bretton Woods Accord, making cost forecasting, investments and revenues a nightmare), the corporate ownership structure dramatically changed. Under the impulse of "raiders" like Milken in the 1980s, classical business were forced to return much higher yields. This was another change in the paradigm, another environment fluctuation, that started to emerge in the 1980s and was fuelled by liberalisation, privatisation, downsizing of planned economies and globalisation; this change has profoundly affected the corporate ownership structure as the influence of funds has become paramount over individual ownership. Again controlling adjusted this new fluctuation and change in paradigm through the development of finer management accounting and business analysis techniques.

This has given birth, inter alia, to the activity based costing (ABC) and later activity based management (ABM) concepts, first described by Johnson and Kaplan during the 1980s (Johnson and Kaplan, 1987). ABC gave a formid-able insight into which parts of the business were profitable and which were not – this was no longer based on the average fixed cost apportioned to the variable activities – and revolutionised the current controlling thinking of the time by putting the activities of the business at the centre of the model.

From this point onwards, the corporation that adopted this new controlling and management costing approach soon produced more than average profits (e.g., Scania), in spite of fluctuating conditions and unpredictable environment.

One of the most advanced control tool is the balanced score card (BSC). BSC is conceptually a sort of flight panel or dashboard, where all relevant information needed for action are displayed.

The key point is relevance. It must be relevant at each level from the very top aggregated eagle's view down to the operating business process owner. Thus, the connection, i.e., the cause to effect loop/link must be clearly evidenced. The management cascade must also be designed in a way that the output of one department becomes the input for the next and so on and so forth.

Balance is the other key point. It means that this dashboard does not only display the tachymeter (the speed), it also displays other key information in a balanced way based on the strategy, e.g., the profit level (tachymeter), the revenues level (speedometer, number of revolutions), the order intake (the tank reserve), the quality index (mileage to go), the client satisfaction index (the outside temperature) and the employees satisfaction (the energy level).

Immediately one sees that the BSC can only hold a limited number of usable indicators. And these indicators need not be financial; they may be, all the more better, physical or statistical.

Summary

Controlling is an old "science", just as old as mankind. Suffice to say that the first ever scripts were Mesopotamian inventory cattle logs on clay tablets, proving that not only the concept of perpetual inventory was mastered, but controlling and monitoring were key management levers. This was 5500 years ago. Since then, sophistications have been brought into the concepts and tools to confront the ever-changing economic and business challenges.

A quantum leap has been achieved in the20th century when controlling moved from audit to the most advanced forecasting- and scenario-based dynamic modelling.

The 21st century challenges have names: inter-nationalisation, cross-cultural management, sustainable performance and eco-performance/management.

A revolution is dawning over controllers, executives and directors which is discussed in Chapters 8 and 9 of this book.

References

Fayol, H. (1917), *Administration Générale et Industrielle.*
Hammer, M. and Champy, J. (1993), *Re-engineering the Corporation.*
Johnson, H.T. and Kaplan, R. (1987), *Relevance Lost.*

The different business-controlling models according to the different phases of internationalisation process/dynamics

This chapter analyses the types and modes of business controlling as well as the ways of business monitoring which are generally commensurate with, and are appropriate to a staged international business development.

To simplify we will always take the perspective of the "outbound" business, i.e., the development from domestic to international, knowing that the opposite flow (i.e., using foreign suppliers in producing goods to be delivered to the domestic market) is just the mirror situation.

Outsourcing and off shoring will be discussed separately.

International development of a business is generally divided into three consecutive phases or stages (Lemaire, 1998) which may overlap over time:

(1) The "first landing"
(2) The "go native"
(3) The multinationalisation.

Most of the time this staged development can be correlated with the firm's growth in size. Small and medium enterprises (SMEs) start with simple export operations and then grow in size, establish a subsidiary abroad to supply to a foreign market, which, over time, may turn into manufacturing and then resells to the group creating an intricate multinational web flow of goods, services and financial transactions.

3.1 From the "first landing" phase to the "go native" phase of dynamic internationalisation

The initial phase, called "first landing", corresponds to the stage where a company contemplates exporting its goods (or services) and "lands" them, for the first time in a foreign market. This management decision can be driven by different considerations, but is mainly the result of the following three main factors:

Excess or unused domestic capacity makes management think that they have overestimated their domestic market at a given moment of time and consider that export is the answer to "filling up" the manufacturing production, or that the plant has overproduced and the excess production could be sold abroad.

Incremental costing is the second most common factor. It works in combination with the preceding. Owing to the fact that the fixed manufacturing costs and administrative overheads have already been absorbed by the regular domestic production, the export-related production is seen as "only" an incremental cost to the firm. Incrementally meaning only the extra variable costs (material, labour, utilities, logistics, etc.).

Testing the waters, the marketing intuition at work – either the domestic market is maturing or is already overmatured and export is seen as a natural geographical expansion, using the same manufacturing and technological base; or management has the "intuition" that there is a market out there for the goods or services and export is a possibility to "test the waters".

After the market abroad has been proved to be secured, a regular export flow is introduced, eventually leading to setting up a local trading subsidiary.

What are the most common steps in the very first steps of the trading subsidiary?

What is at stake, the ad hoc organisations or the role and tasks of the international controller?

The most common sequence is

Exports
Use of a representative office
Use of an agent
Use of a distributor
Establish a reselling local subsidiary.

3.1.1 Export

Is the very first move abroad, as discussed earlier, a "discrete operation" or a series of discrete operations most of the time? At that stage, the focus is mainly on getting the goods landed and getting paid.

Getting the goods landed means paying particular attention to controlling incoterms (international commercial terms) which are issued by the International Chamber of Commerce (ICC) and endorsed by the

United Nations. They specify in detail as to who is responsible for paying for what at which stage and who bears which kind of responsibility. This is a form of internationally agreed best practice that is upheld and respected by international law.

It is important to get a brief understanding and practice of these terms because the cost difference may be significant. Pro memoria the latest issue, the "incoterm 2000" goes from "ex works/EXW" to "free on board/ FOB" to "cost insurance Freight/CIF", etc. The cost difference can vary significantly between the terms and has to be precisely defined before any sales agreement takes place and is built into the export price structure.

Receiving payment can be carried out in a large variety of ways – from a simple bank transfer from the buyer to the most advanced (and complex) documentary credit procedures involving intermediary parties like banks and insurance companies. The general concept underlying the documentary credit is that funds for payment of the goods exported are made available to an intermediary bank which, when it ensures that the goods are effectively delivered through a series of ad hoc (and complicated) documents (e.g., bill of lading, shipment certificates and customs documents), ships the local buyer's funds to the exporter.

This system is normally used when there is a low level of confidence between the exporter and its overseas client. It also ensures that the goods received effectively match the order (against documents) and the right amount of funds for the goods is transferred from the importer at that precise moment.

Foreign exchange (FX) is also a key element and driver within the export price structure. Without entering into complex scenarios, the currency chosen for the sale of the goods will be crucial. If you manufacture in the euro zone (and for the sake of simplicity, all your cost components are euro-based) and invoice an overseas customer, in euros, who is in the dollar zone, you do not take any risk if the rate of the dollar falls against the euro. Conversely, the risk and extra costs due to a potential depreciation of the USD versus the Euro are entirely borne by the customer. However, the overseas customer always has the possibility to protect himself, at a cost to himself against this risk either by hedging, forward payment or through multiple other options which would take too long to explain or go into detail in this book.

The role of controlling is definitely focused on contractual terms, documentary credit and incoterms and FX monitoring. This is done in close link with the export, logistics and sales team. Special care is given to working capital on this point.

3.1.2 Representative office

Using or creating a representative office is not a compulsory phase, but often proves to be a useful one, namely, for sizable businesses, e.g., project work, engineering and tenders., where it is important to have a permanent presence abroad from a sales and marketing point of view. The role of the representative office is to watch the local market closely, including the latest development in trends, competition, prices, product and service offerings. It also enables market intelligence and provides a presence to respond quickly to public or private tenders (e.g., in consulting or civil engineering projects) and pro-actively fosters new opportunities. In other words, the role of the representative office is marketing. The representative office is not a resale subsidiary or an agent: its role is not to perform sales stricto sensu. The actual sales are performed by the parent company back in homeland as export sales. The representative office is purely set up as a cost centre, where costs accumulate and no revenue ever passes through. Periodically, the parent company abroad would cover these costs and replenish its bank account.

The typical cost elements of a representative office are office space, telecoms, travelling- and personal costs.

Consequently, the controller's focus should be on cost control (versus budget) and on what is gained out of this cost centre, i.e., volume and quality of business intelligence, number of sales leads, numbers of bids and tenders responded or completed and volume and intensity of prospect visits to assess the cost–benefit relationship.

3.1.3 Use of an agent

A sales agent as defined here is a person or a business who acts as a representative of the parent company and who negotiates sales without taking title deed of the goods, as the agent does not actually purchase the goods to resell them, but acts on behalf of the manufacturer or parent service provider.

The task that an agent performs on behalf of the parent company is one that a marketing and sales department would normally perform, but in a foreign country. More specifically it consists of deploying all the necessary marketing intelligence and sales push to increase the sales of the products it represents.

However, when a local deal is made by the sales agent representing the firm back in the homeland, the goods are directly shipped and invoiced by the parent company to the local customer who in turn pays the parent company, more or less as described in the "export" case.

The sales agent's remuneration is aimed at

Covering its costs
Making a profit.

Both elements are combined in a commission structure based on the sales achieved (or as variants on invoices actually paid, revenues billed, order intake, etc.), most of the time by means of a percentage scheme.

The controller's role in that is to monitor the effective "agency" activity versus cost

That is, the services paid for via the commission rates are effectively rendered. It is important to get a clear statement of what means are deployed specifically to support the marketing of the parent company's goods. In majority of the cases the agent is not exclusive, but represents other local or exporting firms in the same country, be they from a similar industrial sector or from different sectors. The company's marketing and promotional resources are shared amongst several players. Controlling the effort dedicated specifically to the export company's products is key in terms of the number of product managers (or fraction of time of product managers) assigned to view, e.g., the number of specific client visits, number of trade shows and fairs attended, amount and quality of sales into the market – including price competition and distribution, as well as competitor's promotion structures and market intelligence. This quantitative evaluation of the marketing support given by the agent to the export company's products will therefore form the basis of the costs that need to be covered, and thus the percentage commission that can be allocated to the actual sales performed. In most cases this objective calculation is "forgotten" when renegotiating commission at the time of contract renewal; this is because both parties tend to focus on percentage points and increments (or decrement) versus the former period, but more seldom on the actual function performed.

It is also important for the controller to note that a signed contractual agreement between an exporting company and that of a local sales agent will be governed, for the most part, under the local law of that country. There may also be other risks to take into consideration, such as protection for the local agent under local law and indemnity payments in case of a rupture of the agent's contract. Careful consideration must be made towards the property rights of the client's customer base. In most European countries, during the time of the contract between the two parties and sometimes over and above this period even when the agent is no longer active, this remains the property of the local agent, thus the export company cannot sell in the absence of the agent by shipping goods directly to clients without the agent's consent or paying a commission to the agent.

Elements of the working capital

The accounts receivables and the related days sales outstanding (DSOs)
The inventory level.

The FX: exposure and coverage policy

As part of the parent company's obligations (the principal) there are three *fundamental elements* that need to be provided to an agent if the relationship is not only to be balanced but also efficient.

Training must be provided by the company if it wishes to see its products successfully sold in the market. The scope of training and updating ranges for new products/technology, new promotion techniques and demonstration kits, including all the novelties that must be known by the agent to ensure that the agent remains competitive for the company's products, with the best chances to win new business and increase the current business, must be taken into consideration. Again, in the field, this kind of self-understanding support is very often neglected by the principal exporting company, which can prove to be ultimately detrimental.

Marketing support must also be provided. The cost of the marketing support is to be borne by the principal (parent company). This is a matter of negotiation and must be addressed early on during the initial negotiations and built into the agreement to determine the commission percentages. For example, a 7% commission on sales billed would leave enough margin to cover the costs of two fully paid full-time local product managers, dedicated to promoting the parent company's business locally. Conversely, the parent company commits itself to launching an advertising campaign twice a year in the local market (specifying in detail the budget allocated to the type of media to be used, etc.) to support its products and the agent's effort and to create a sufficient "pull" effect.

Management systems and support must be fed into the sales order information to establish a smooth supply chain. Parts of these management systems are budgeting, reporting and deviation/trend monitoring tools.

Although this is not stricto sensu an obligation which is governed by law, in the frame of a principal–agent relationship, it is none the less essential that this information exchange and action monitoring does exist in practice. A very simple example is when a proper budget is put together between the principal (parent company) and the agent; the production, packaging and material planning have higher chances of being carried out smoothly, and so does the shipping and the inventory planning.

Summary

Strengths
Light structure
Work on a properly calculated commission basis or "paid when paid" basis

Permanent local market presence/push

No upfront capital investment

Local market intelligence

Excellent for first time to market experience and low volume sales.

Weaknesses

No strong commitment (multiple representation, if non-exclusive, one amongst others)

Perceived as a remote player

Sometimes weak loyalty

Not the in-house drive

Lags behind

No corporate element

Weak or absent management control.

Controls

Budget

Sales performed, order in take register

Costs, as a portion of the commission, in line with actual resources committed/dedicated?

Reporting

Principal/agent terms of reference/contract type

Market analysis/information.

3.1.4   Use of a distributor

On glancing, the use of a distributor could appear similar to or even just another word for an agent. However, this is certainly not true. There is a huge difference between an agent as defined earlier and a distributor. A distributor, as defined, actually purchases the goods and therefore takes title to the goods to resell them, in general, into the local market. The distributor is therefore the prime customer contact in the sales chain for the principal exporting parent company.

In practice, this significantly changes the nature of the relationship as well as the methods of controlling and monitoring.

In the first instance, the profit construction changes dramatically whereas in the case of the agent there is a commission on sales to

(a)   cover the agents costs engaged to push the company's products;
(b)   provide for his net profit margin.

In the case of the distributor, a "discount" is offered based on the merchant's market price that will allow for his

(a)   own administrative and marketing costs;
(b)   inventory handling and own logistic costs;
(c)   profit margin;
(d)   promotion and marketing costs (of which, under a specific framework of negotiation, a fraction of the corporate element is to be borne by the parent company);
(e)   administrative costs – the fraction that can be allocated to the parent company's business;
(f)   FX risk, or cost of risk coverage.

In practice, this clearly means that doing business through a distributor is more complex than working with and supporting an agent. Again the distributor may or may not be exclusive. Using the same theoretical example (cf table) as before it can be seen that a 7% commission given to an agent taking all other things as being equal, is roughly equivalent to a 15% discount given to a distributor to achieve a comparable job. In practice, depending on countries and business sectors, it can be as high as 50–60% (e.g., clothing).

Owing to the different structure between an agent and a distributor, the net profit level of both is not expected to be identical. It is recognised that profit levels will vary depending on the level of risk and entrepreneurship. The more entrepreneurial and/or the higher the risks taken by the distributor, or the higher the business risk is, the more rewarding it should be (high risk/high return ratio) and thus the higher the profit level.

In the case of exporting, the position of the distributor is clearly more risky and entrepreneurial than that of an agent. The distributor takes the risk to buy the goods upfront, by the same token, as inventory from the exporter and takes the full risk if the goods do not sell, do not fit into the market, or there is a situation of overbuys, etc. The distributor thus has to advance working capital to finance the purchases, and usually for much larger volumes as set out in an agreement, even for a minimum order quantity that has to be purchased at every order or spread over the contractual year to maintain a good discount. The distributor usually pays for promotion and marketing costs, etc. of the products too.

It is therefore normal that his share of net profit margin should be higher, 4% or more as in our example; in practice, it would vary depending on circumstances and countries of destination.

Keeping in mind that this profit margin belongs to the distributors, it can be increased if the business is managed well by reducing direct and/ or fixed costs. However, poor management or bad control of logistics or a weak hedging policy could wipe out any expected profit margin.

The question remains as to what makes it attractive to work through a distributor as opposed to an agent

Basically the answer to this question is twofold.

Firstly, in majority of cases the answer is linked to size of business flow and the complexity of goods. The bigger the business and the more complex the products working through a distributor are, the better it is because a more strong and visible structure is available; the agent is generally of a more elusive nature.

Secondly, there are some businesses and countries where business needs go through a fixed local legal entity. For example, an exporter exporting goods to the defence industry in France has to go through a registered incorporated company agreed by the state. This is especially the case for non-EU member state exporting companies.

The same applies in case of tenders, where to respond and compete one needs to have a local legal shell with local staffing (sometimes a local manpower content is required). This is particularly true for systems or engineering or civil engineering projects.

The controller's role

The controller's role is to monitor the following.

Sales volume

This appears obvious, but sometimes neglected. The volume of goods sold is a robust indicator of a good or bad trend.

Order intake

This is probably the best precursor of a trend regardless of which industrial sector the company may be involved with. It allows the controller to get an early "feel" for the business development, and hopefully gives enough time to make any necessary adjustments.

Market price

Any discounts on the market price that has been agreed with a distributor, or agent shows the functions actually performed by the distributor and his commitment level.

Deciding the market price in foreign markets is always difficult and sometimes it bears no resemblance to the domestic market.

Mini case: French Cosmetics in Asia

A French cosmetics manufacturer, in southern France, was pricing its good intrinsic quality products in the French middle market, and was selling some of them via "health stores" in supermarkets. When it started exporting to Korea, Japan and China, it opened a branch office in Paris to ensure that the word "Paris" could be clearly visible on the packaging. Passing the product through Paris "marketing" allowed him to triple the product's selling price, making it and its distributors happy when compared with the domestic market; the "Paris brand" is a powerful sales aid for a certain category of products, especially in the luxury sector.

The Korean, Japanese and Chinese distributors were very active in obtaining the necessary authorisation of the cosmetics through the respective health authorities, a pre-requisite to ensure that the products could be sold in the market, because the distributors knew the detailed mechanisms of these procedures.

Mini case: The Liberty Jeep in France

The Liberty Jeep is positioned as a medium-range SUV/off-road in the United States, and being priced at around 20 000 USD domestically in 2007, it is often purchased for a student or as a second car for the family. In France, however, the very same "Liberty Jeep", called "Cherokee", would be positioned "upscale" and priced at 32 000 euros (45 000 USD). Doubling the retail price is not just a matter of logistical costs for European specifications, but it is a result of different product positioning which allows higher margins to be shared between the manufacturer in Toledo, the United States and the local importer.

Budget

A budget made with the distributor or by the distributor is a mandatory business control element. It is highly recommended to have a clause in the distributorship agreement that provides for this budgeting exercise. The simple reason is that working through a distributor is an engaging decision and both parties must be committed towards a certain level of business generation. It guarantees the exporter a minimum visibility on the future sales which allows for dedicated resources to be committed, such as dedicated packaging and labels (translations), adapting products to fit local regulations, and specific manufacturing scheduling. If, e.g., export packaging is different from domestic packaging, then export production for a specific or several batch has to be planned; for which tools, equipment and the supply chain have to be adjusted well in advance.

From a distributor's point of view, the advantage of having a budget ensures the distributor with guaranteed levels, ranges and time slots for manufactured products that would be sent on time to the distributor for resale in the local foreign market.

Rolling forecast

This is another key monitoring element in the exporter–distributor relationship. If the distributor and the exporter have agreed on a business budget (aforementioned), for instance, on a yearly basis, it will be important to schedule this business based on production time and shipment weeks.

In this case, the distributor is bound to inform the exporter through a monthly report:

(a) Its past and current month's performance
Its following expected sales (over the next 6 months for instance) and consequently orders to the exporter/manufacturer of which the first 2 months are considered as firm orders, and the third month as 70% (for example) firm.

(b) Its roll over month over month
It is important to consider the first "months" of the rolling forecast as firm orders but the remaining from 70% firm to indicative because the rolling forecast is the tool that will allow manufacturing to plan ahead and forecast the promotion material to be ready and translated on time.

The discount factor

It is clear that the distributor's margin is calculated as a discount factor based on the local market price. As in case of the agent, it is important to link this discount factor to the support and resources specifically dedicated to the exporter's products. However, it might prove to be quite difficult to reach this level of transparency since the distributor is, technically, a legal entity separate from the exporter/principal. In this respect, the distributor is not bound/obliged to open up his books to what is just a supplier (i.e., the exporter) for him/her. It is totally an arms length transaction. In practice the "open book" is either part of a specific provision in the distributorship agreement, or is a matter of negotiation and a goodwill relationship. It is needless to say that the first case is best, but it is not feasible always – not only because it is not at the distributor's advantage, but also because it depends on the relative bargaining power between the exporter and the local distributor. Also, according to local corporate legislations, the caveat should be such that a "look through" mechanism coupled with a monitoring and controlling system lead to make the distributor, de facto, legally controlled (even though there is no stake in the share capital) by the exporter, and in case of troubles (like bankruptcy or product liability) the damages could also extend to the exporter in solidum.

Logistics

It goes without saying that monitoring the international logistics loop is one of the most critical steps. Most of the time export goods are not similar to the goods in the domestic market. They can vary considerably in conception or nature. This is often the case with champagnes or spirits that are treated differently in terms of taste and sweetness based on their country of destination. The packaging of the products also may vary extensively from domestic to export, in terms of size, openings, safety regulations, etc. And most of the time the labelling is different with regard to translations and specific brand names.

Mini case: Brand names – a localisation is often needed

A top American car manufacturer manufactured a medium-range car that sold well in the United States under the brand name Nova. It then exported this car to Latin America under the same name, and contrary to its expectations the car did not sell well. The reason was the perception of the name that was very negative: "Nova" literally means "it does not work!" in Spanish. And no one wanted to buy a car self-proclaiming that it would not work. The same occurred with a Japanese car, the MR2, selling brilliantly in the United States and the United Kingdom. However, for the French market the name had to be changed from MR2 to just MR. In French, MR2 (merdeux) sounds phonetically like the word "shitty", and no French person wanted to be seen driving a "shitty" car.

This is why a specific logistical chain has to be set up and monitored carefully; the rolling forecast being pivotal in this process.

Working capital

In this case the working capital can be focused on two elements.

The receivables balance, materialised by the DSOs
The DSOs are not to be confused with overdues. For example, a 178 days for a DSO might not be overdue because the contractual payment terms specify 180 days net with this specific country's distributor, whereas a 37 DSOs might be overdue by 7 days if the terms with the distributor in another country specify 30 days net.

A DSO's range can differ considerably throughout Europe from 10 days in Nordic countries, to 30 in Switzerland, 33 in Germany, 112 in France, 168 in Spain and over 180 in Greece. It corresponds to both a cultural attitude and the structure of the credit and banking systems of each country.

The inventory level, materialised by the Days Sales of Inventory
The inventory level at the exporter's company or warehouse is a control point to monitor to make sure that the working capital is kept at minimum. The inventory level at the distributor level is virtually impossible to control as it belongs to the distributor, not the exporter.

Foreign exchange
It is equally important and is to be managed as is the case with an agent.

Summary

Strengths
Locally entrepreneurial established structure
A single selling point
Visible permanent presence
Product local availability at all times thorough obligation to have local inventories
Excellent local market intelligence
Good, to excellent support (technology, administrative, etc.)
Fit for large volumes
Can take stock thus be quicker with immediate sales into the market (just in time deliveries).

33

Weaknesses

Less, if no control: command on the local customer (marketing is made through the distributor)

Cost of doing business may be more expensive

Potentially detrimental if "bad" distributor

Cost of contract breach/change.

Controls

Local market prices

Budgets and rolling forecast, order book

Discount given versus resources committed

DSOs

Inventory control (DSIs)

Reporting

FX

Marketing intelligence.

3.1.5 Local reselling subsidiary

In the former paragraphs, we have looked at the phase where a company starts its international development via export operations. Most of the time this corresponds to a small and growing activity that Jean Paul Lemaire terms "the first landing" phase, where goods were landed outside the domestic borders for the first time (Lemaire ,1998).

It was done by working through a representative agent or a distributor, without having to establish a permanent base abroad.

At some point in time, the exporter will be confronted with the choice of opening up a full-fledged foreign resale/trading subsidiary in the form of a standalone company, where the parent company is the shareholder, incorporated under the foreign country's laws where the goods are traded.

The foreign subsidiary's role is to pro-actively foster outlets for goods that the parent company is manufacturing and to sell them in the local market, by buying them from the parent company and importing them (Figure 3.1).

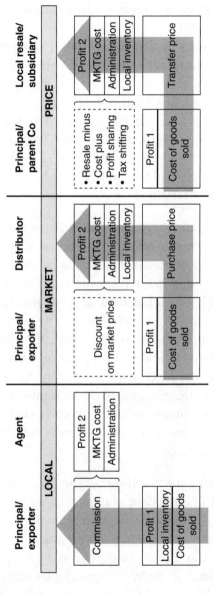

Figure 3.1 Principal to Agent: economic functions performed and remuneration models.

Interestingly enough, in economic terms, the foreign resale subsidiary functions identically to that of a distributor

So why choose to set up a foreign trading subsidiary instead of working through a distributor?
This is no easy answer. As a general rule, a subsidiary (sub) is a better option as it goes along with growth and size: the bigger the volume of business, the more reasons to create the foreign sub. If this axiom tends to be true more often than not, it is not necessary always true, and therefore there is no automatic answer. The best way to look at it is from a pure, economic rationale. In other words, is it economically more efficient to set up and run a sub than it is to use a distributor from a managerial perspective (Do we handle local business better?) and then assess the cost–benefit relation?

The foreign trading subsidiary has one major advantage: it belongs to the parent company and therefore it can reasonably be assumed that it will run exclusively in accordance with the parent company's interests. A distributor, on the other hand, (especially in the case of non-exclusive distributor) will put his own business interests first (and the whole difficulty is to maximise the alignment between the interests of the exporter with those of the distributor, whilst using incentives like granting advantageous discount factors) and has to spread his resources on many other brands/business to push them at the same time. This dilutes management control and allows a lack of direct handling on critical aspects of the marketing mix coupled with the effective cost–benefit calculation of the discount factors granted which are very often the drivers to set a foreign trading sub in motion.

In terms of controlling and monitoring the business, it is substantially different. The local involvement is much higher since the personnel is local, with possibly some expatriates in functions that require a deep understanding of the parent company's systems, technology or products. It means that the human resources and administration are local, and so are the personnel costs, in compliance with local reporting to GAAP and tax regulations. So this creates a burden of local costs which should on an average be less, if the structure was done through a local distributor, stressing again the importance to really establish a serious cost–benefit before making this choice.

Having made this point, it must be said that the bulk of foreign subsidiary costs are not the administrative support costs, neither the sales nor marketing costs, but are the cost of goods sold.

The cost of goods sold is the pivotal element in a foreign trading subsidiary, it constitutes transfer price

Although the basic decision of setting up this local structure is to bring the goods from parent company into a market to sell them locally, with hopefully better economic and financial conditions than through a distributor, the price at which the parent company will sell them to its subsidiary will directly and heavily determine the local profit (or loss) level of the foreign subsidiary (in relation, of course, to the local market price).

Also note that the profit level of the foreign subsidiary will be taxed according to local legislation, and thus determining the price at which the goods are sold from parent company to the foreign subsidiary will have a tax dimension.

Furthermore, it is not a game where one can freely adjust the selling price between the parent company and the subsidiary just for the sake of shifting the profit in the country (either the homeland of the parent company or the foreign country) where the most attractive (lower) corporate tax rate exists.

Either way, both the home and the foreign tax authorities will be extremely vigilant to make sure that their "fair" share of taxes does not escape their hands (Figure 3.2).

The *transfer prices* are therefore not a totally "sovereign" decision but are governed by polices and frame rules, which are set by acceptable practices globally.

The *OECD* (Organisation for Economic Co-operation and Development), in 1979, is the first to have "codified" this practice within the "Transfer Pricing Guidelines for Multinational Enterprises and Tax Authorities" which is regularly updated.

The *United Nations* Commission on Trade and Development (UNCTAD) issued a policy paper in 1999 on "Transfer Pricing", and the *EU* commission regularly issues policies and guidelines on the subject,

In moneraty terms

	Agent	Distributor	Resale subsidiary
Market price	100	100	100
Sales force	3	3	3 to 10
Promotion	1	1	1
Marketing	1	2	1
Administration	NA	1	1 to 2
Inbound logistics	NA	1	1
Unventory	NA	1	1
Outbound logistics	NA	1	1
FX cost/risk	NA	1	1
Profit element	2	4	2 to 4
Total	7	15	10
	Commission 7%	Discount 15% of the market price	Local cost 10–18% Local sub profit 2–4%

Figure 3.2 Cost/function performed principal/agent.

namely, via its "EU joint Transfer pricing Forum" in 2004. The IRS (Inland Revenue Service), the US tax authority and the US Bureau of Customs and Border Protection also issue guidelines and rules, although they conflict with each other in some instances.

Without getting into the details on tax-related mechanisms of transfer pricing, in this book, following are some basic robust and generally admitted principles which stem from the OECD guidelines.

The *overriding concept* to be tax compliant (i.e., not deliberately shifting profit from a country to another to avoid taxes) is that a transaction between a parent company and its subsidiary must be done at "arm's length". This means that the parent company should/must deal with its own subsidiary as if it was a totally independent economical entity (which it is from a legal point of view anyway: the subsidiary is a distinct entity from the parent company).

In practice, the OECD guidelines provide a global framework or rules and policies to achieve this. Following are the most commonly used:

Comparables
Cost plus

Resale minus
Profit sharing
TNM/CPM/APA.

Without going into the minute detailed analysis of each method (there are specialised books and memoranda on the subject), here is a quick overview of the strengths and weaknesses of each.

Comparables

The idea here is to find the most exact comparable pricing on the merchant market by using open market transactions, i.e., the comparison of the sale of goods to a distributor by a manufacturer other than the parent company of exact comparable goods. Therefore, the"fair market price" that should be used between the parent company and subsidiary transaction is the same price that exists between the comparable exporter and independent distributor transaction.

Strengths
Theoretically, it is a perfect benchmark.

Weaknesses
In practice it is quasi-impossible to realise, because rarely are the same goods traded by both an independent exporter to a distributor and the parent company to its subsidiary. In any case, identical circumstances never exist.

Cost plus

The idea is that the market price on the local market is calculated by accumulating successive costs strata, manufacturing, logistics, import taxes, advertising, overhead share, etc. plus a "fair margin" to remunerate the work/functioning of the local subsidiary.

Strengths
- It remains an easy way to build up a price structure: applying a mark-up to a cost base is both intuitive and looks rational.
- Easy to administrate.

- Fits well with engineering and project work, tenders and bids, work to order (power plants, transports systems, aeronautics, defence systems etc.).

Weaknesses

Theoretically it is a very logical idea but often, by simply adding costs and margins to arrive at a local price, the end result is far superior to the level of prices that would be acceptable in the local market. This is frequently the case when exporting from a high cost base, such as Switzerland, to lower purchasing power countries such as Africa. The danger of this method is to price the goods completely out of the market. This also creates a FX exposure as, de facto, the domestic currency represents the vast majority of the cost content.

Getting a clear view on the constitutive costs of a product, especially when it comes to allocating overheads and fixed costs to a specific product, is a problem. Apart from the Activity Based Costing (ABC) method, all other cost allocating methods introduce biases and flaws in the product costing. This can be a major problem both ways:

(a) Either the product is underloaded with costs, thus the fixed costs are not recuperated although the margins made from the international sale appears optically correct. This appears very often when only the variable or direct costs are taken into consideration.

(b) Or the costs are too heavily loaded, i.e., they take on too large a proportion of the overheads which do not contribute to their developments, and therefore the products outprice themselves; thus obliging an "open book" policy which might cause problem with other global competitors that could "sneak-into" manufacturing costs and supplier base.

Resale minus

The resale minus method is exactly the opposite of the cost plus. This starts from the local market price fit for the product. This is the most fair as it is market-based, thus by definition, competing with all other local suppliers, all other things being equal.

The calculation then works in reverse order; it deducts a margin from the market price, expressed as a percentage of the selling price, which is intended to remunerate the local trading subsidiary for its sales and marketing function, in such a way that, finally, the Earnings Before Income Tax (EBIT) of the resale subsidiary may range from 2% to 4% of its turnover.

Strengths

- Very intuitive and market-driven, thus given an edge to the local subsidiary to compete on the local market.
- Flexible at the subsidiary level.
- "Almost" guarantees a profit level commensurate to the local subsidiary's economic function.
- Fits well with fast-moving goods, typically consumer goods (consumer electronics, luxury goods, light arms, etc.)

Weaknesses

This method "pushes" the pressure onto the parent company and the transfer price, calculated from the market price minus a discount factor, might turn out to be inferior to the cost of manufacturing the goods; thus leaving a "loss" in the parent company's books, although the subsidiary might be making a profit (2–4%).

Since this method is market-based, it may cause a substantial amount of fluctuations; thus creating a multiple transfer price for the same item. This could result in an exposure to tax authorities as in most cases, if not all circumstances, the tax authorities look for consistency and stability in the transfer prices.

Not easy to administrate in practice.

Note:

- The pragmatic "rule" is that once a method is chosen it is not advisable to change it (consistency rule).
- Regardless of the method chosen, keeping traces of all documentation is necessary to be able to trace back the price formation in a consistent way and over time.
- Within a range of products, a minimum consistency in margins or mark-ups must be kept, unless there are specific sound reasons to deviate, such as product launches or phasing a product out.

Profit sharing

Although recognised as a method by the OECD guidelines, profit sharing (or profit split) is neither conceptually efficient, nor workable in practice.

Conceptually, it is hard to work at arm's length and share the profit between two parties (the parent company and the subsidiary) at the same time. Would it be realistic to share profit at real arm's length with a client?

In practice, it is extremely complicated to define the "total" profit of a product throughout the global value-added chain, and then split it according to the different stages – the resale foreign subsidiary being one amongst other elements in the whole chain of the transfer pricing.

APA

Advance Pricing Agreement (APA), vis à vis the IRS, is becoming more "fashionable" in the United States and among the EU member states.

The concept here is that a global corporation will seek an advance "ruling" before engaging in a trade with its foreign trading subsidiary. Prices set with the approval from the related countries' tax authorities (given in advance), provided these prices are followed in practice, results in no tax exposure existing any longer.

Mini case: When APA Rhymes with APEX

Theoretically, the APA's rules vary widely from one country to the other. The IRS, e.g., is very keen in working out a theoretical profit for the whole global value added and then splitting it among all the elements of the VA according to their relative merits, e.g., the parent company which is doing the R&D and manufacturing is due to have a higher share of the whole global profit commensurate for its "entrepreneurial" economic function, whereas its resale foreign subsidiary will be "allotted" a smaller profit share according to its more modest economic role of only selling the product in the market.

Theoretically, it is a very complex concept to grasp, as the vast majority of this is almost a direct theoretical application of macroeconomics to business, where we now know that these theories can seldom be applied to macroeconomics and business economics. There is as much difference as it is between the relativity theory and quantum physics. The former applies to the large-scale (macro) environment and the latter to small-scale environment (businesses). Similarly, the way they both explain the physical world, in which we live, is not compatible with one another.

In practice, it is extremely hard to quantify and cumbersome to achieve as the information systems are not naturally geared to deliver this kind of information within companies. In fact it is a large amount of information to produce, to track over the past years and maintain all the way into the future, over and above the normal business information. When an APA was carried out for a prominent Swiss multinational with its US subsidiary, it not only took 2 years to complete, but also triggered a full-scale IRS audit before the APA would eventually be granted. When the APA was finally signed, the company had by then been absorbed and reorganised by a German conglomerate, and the whole exercise had to be started all over from scratch with the new merged product lines.

Controls

Parent Co	Foreign trading subsidiary
	Marketing intelligence
	Market share
	Local market prices
	Budgets rolling forecast, order book
Transfer Prices	Transfer prices
	DSOs
	Inventory control (DSIs)
Reporting ROS	Reporting ROS
FX	FX
	Headcount
	Profit level (2–4%)

3.2 From the "go native" to the "multinational" phase

There are two distinct phases in this process: creating a local manufacturing company and creating a web of local companies (trading or manufacturing) which not only trade in a foreign market but also within the international network of the corporation. This ultimate phase is called multinationalisation.

3.2.1 The local manufacturing company

The purpose:

There are multiple reasons for creating a local manufacturing corporation. In most cases, there are two key drivers:

(1) To do business with a specific country, it is necessary to have a local manufacturing company because either it is specified by local law (the legal argument); or it is uneconomical to import (customs taxes being prohibitively high on imports, they would price the products out of the local market – e.g., Brazil). The reason being in both cases to protect the local entrepreneurs and/or protecting local employment.

(2) The parent company wants to take advantage of local manufacturing conditions such as
   – low labour costs (Vietnam and India – call centres)
   – superior manufacturing quality (Switzerland – watches)
   – superior engineering quality (Bangalore – software)
   – image connected with the country (Paris – fragrance and fashion).

In terms of controls, the manufacturing subsidiaries are a totally different set-up to the purely trading resale subsidiaries.

All the classical parameters traditionally connected with the manufacturing environment will be found, over and above the different controls, levers, and monitoring systems that have been discussed in the earlier sections, i.e.,

Materials
Labour

Utilities
Engineering
Energy
Supply chain and logistics
FX
Taxes.

Without going into the details on ways to control a manufacturing facility per se, since this is not the main purpose of this book and is discussed in detail in specific publications and other books, more emphasis will be on the specific international perspectives.

In the perspective where a foreign manufacturing subsidiary is established due to legal reasons, there is not much space for manoeuvre – except just to do it.

However, the cost–benefit balance must be kept in mind when the reason to establish a local manufacturing subsidiary is to take advantage of the local operating conditions. This may seem obvious, but is actually under-considered in practice.

Mini case: American petrochemical's investment in Europe

A leading US chemical company used to trade-in Adiponotrile (precursor to nylon salts) via its long-established resale subsidiaries in Europe.

However, by the end of the 1970s, the USD, compared with all the other European currencies, was so high (almost 9 French francs to 1 USD) that it was virtually impossible to sell any more by exporting to Europe.

This led the American chemical giant to establish a gigantic joint venture manufacturing facility in France with a French chemical company manufacturing through the former's latest technology under licence to serve the whole of the European market.

The construction time took 2 years for the new facility in east of France, which was extremely fast, given the circumstances in the region and the cost of 1 billion USD.

By the time this brand new facility was finished and had produced its first ton of Adiponotrile, the USD/French franc parity was down to 3 French francs for 1 USD. In other words, the irony was – now that all the cost component were French-based, it was a better deal to import again through the resale subsidiary!

Moreover, its French joint venture partner in the meantime had been "nationalised" under the newly elected social communist administration, resulting in 50% of the partnership being nationalised under the French government. The latter had its views about profit planning, cash flows, human resources (called "politique sociale" in French), dividend policies, tax planning, etc.

The foregoing case shows how important it is to make the decision of switching from importing via a resale subsidiary to manufacturing locally. It is neither light nor an easy decision to make. Most of the decision models are based on economic equations and financial simulations that are in essence "static". Although they are "painted" dynamic, they are in fact not. This leaves a portion of risk in the decision making that cannot be avoided regardless of all the possible calculations and simulations.

The new EADS (Airbus, etc.) management is to take a similar decision regarding where to localise the manufacturing facilities in the world and possibly move them out of Europe into dollarised regions. The cost of Airbuses is euro-based whereas the selling price is USD dominated. Until a couple of years ago (2005) the parity was 0.70 euro to 1 USD; now (2007) it is 1.5 euro to 1 USD.

The idea of making use of advantageous local conditions is almost as old as economics itself. It is clearly at the centre of Adam Smith's 1776 (Smith, 1776) seminal book: *An Enlightenment in the Nature and the Cause of the Wealth of the Nations*; Adam Smith founded the "free" trade concept, also termed "liberalism".

The basic principle being that every nation has things that they are good at doing (they have a competitive advantage) and things that they are not good at (resource is scarce or skill is absent). Therefore, it seemed obvious to focus only on those things that a nation is good at doing and produce them in mass and trade them internationally, ignoring the other things that the nation cannot do well.

However, actually putting this into practice is not easy due to its sociological (dislocation of otherwise comprehensive human societies, shift of paradigm from local societal/moral values to universal monetary value), ecological (travel of goods on long distance around the globe, using up fossil fuels and emitting CO_2) and economical (constant impoverishment of already poor countries over the past centuries, i.e., not having the "right" resources), amongst many other, aspects.

As far as controlling and monitoring are concerned, two major dimensions must be kept in mind.

Firstly, the initial evaluation phase is to decide on the foreign investment to build a local manufacturing facility. This includes the FX (on the foreseeable long range), political conditions, tax policies (e.g., consistency in dividends repatriation for example), infrastructure and all other conditions that are key elements to appraise. Equally important is the availability of local resources, energy, utilities and employment because it would be too late to change after the investment is made; although these elements still need monitoring afterwards.

The second point is inherent to the fact that most of the operating controls will be in the hand of the local manufacturing plant. In other words, the vast majority of the value-added/profit-generating capability will be in the hands of the subsidiary; the "lever" of the transfer pricing is no longer there to monitor the bottom line (within a tax acceptable range) from a distance (the parent company) as used to be in the case of the resale subsidiary.

The economic levers that are left are parent company level to influence the local profit level and thus tax levels are as follows:

Management fees: Here the parent company charges fees (1% of the revenues) for management services that are rendered by the parent company to its subsidiary. Among the classical recurring components of the management are the marketing fees (contribution to the international marketing strategy), the administrative fees (IT/IS) the human resources fees, etc.

For management fees to be accepted by the local tax authorities, it is, however, important to keep in mind the following universal concepts (which by definition are not in favour of them as they see them as tax siphoning): they have to be substantial (a real service is rendered) and documented (agreements signed between the parent company and the subsidiary, fees are to be specified in detail, time sheets, etc., all at "arms length" as much as possible). Their value is to be consistent with a "market" value, i.e., what an external consultant would have charged for a similar service, and ultimately they have to benefit the subsidiary directly.

In other words, mere mechanical cost allocations of overheads as a cost spit out of a central computer in the parent company is a recipe for disaster.

Royalties: This element refers to Intellectual Property (IP) rights which has become considerably complex over the recent years.

The very notion of IP is not a self-going concept. Until the beginning of the industrial era it was not an issue. On the contrary, intellectual innovations were not only for free but they had to be disclosed for free too! This paradigm is what kept mankind going from the dawn of civilisation: Plato and Aristotle created institutions, the Academy and the Lyceum, respectively, where they created and disseminated, for free, science and knowledge to all those interested.

This was at peak during the century of Enlightenment, with the first Encyclopedia being put together by the French scientists and philosophers Dalambert and Diderot to make knowledge free and accessible to all.

It is only recently that a profound change of mentality has occurred and knowledge, design, drawing, inventions, names, bacteria, human tissues are all seen as having a monetary value. One can imagine the consequence if a royalty had to be paid to Newton, Euclid, Pascal and Bole today, should this paradigm be applied.

Today, the IP is extremely regulated under the auspices of the UN: the WIPO (World Intellectual Property Office) in Geneva, in connection with WTO (World Trade Organization) also in Geneva which is regulating and arbitrating the implementation of IP rights (TRIPS).

Using someone's IP rights (patent or trade mark or author's right) enforces a payment to be made for this right: this is the royalty. If the parent company has a special R&D or manufacturing "gimmick", which it has duly patented, and allows its foreign subsidiary to use it, as in the foregoing case, then the foreign subsidiary will have to pay a royalty to its parent company in return. Needless to say that the amount of royalties paid to the parent company are under scrutiny by the foreign tax authorities, who may be tempted to disclaim a portion of it if they consider it to be in excess of a reasonable level. In case the amounts are substantial, it is advisable to go thorough an APA (cf supra) exercise.

Mini case: Big pharmaceutical company and its IP on AIDS drugs and other avian flu tablets and human "spare parts"

Recent IP rights – pharmaceuticals IP – were under a heated debate when it was requested to lower the royalties paid on AIDS drugs to make the medicine affordable and available to emerging economies such as southern African countries. The same debate was initiated on the production of an anti-avian flu drug.

Heated discussions take place when it comes to "patent" medication made of human cells or human cells elements that are intended to mend other human organs – spare parts.

In terms of management, controlling a foreign manufacturing subsid-iary means either to "keep" control of the subsidiary through expatriates from the parent company or to leave the "levers" to locally recruited managers and technicians. Both schools of thought have their advantages and dis-advantages, and in practice what is seen is a progressive shift from "all expatriate" to local managers over a period of time, when the operations are moving from a start–up phase to a more mature and secured business.

Summary

Strengths

Takes full advantage of local conditions/resources
Becomes a local "good citizen" and thus has equal access to local tenders as for local players

49

Becomes seen as local when this is a necessary perception by local buyers.

Weaknesses

Heavy and committed long-term investment

Initial economic and financial long-term assumptions may prove wrong within days or months

Loss of operational control from parent company

Driving by wire: distance monitoring

Spreadsheet management: the emphasis moves from the business to the reported image of business through the inflation reports and reports on the variance between consecutive reports.

Controls

Again without going into the detail of those controls which are universal to any manufacturing facility.

FX

Tax

Management fees

Royalties

Reporting: ROS, ROI, ROCE, profit level

Benchmarking

Management.

3.2.2 Multinationalisation

Here there is no change of magnitude but a change of order instead (Figure 3.3).

The macro-economists call it Foreign Direct Investment (FDI) and the phase of multinationalisation is made of multinational corporations called MNCs. The concept of transnational corporations (TNCs) is also used.

Many analyses and surveys have been carried on MNCs and FDIs (mainly the UN, UNCTAD, ILO, OECD, etc.) and it appears that over the 20 biggest economies in the world more than half are MNCs (measured by their

Business-controlling models according to phases of process/dynamics

	First landing		Go native		Multinational-isation	
	Representative office	Agent	Distributor	Resale subsidiaries	Manufacturer subsidiary	MNC
Local pro active marketing	X	X	X	X	X	X
Foster sales	X	X	X	X	X	X
Perform sales		X on behalf	X	X	X	X
Invoice local customer			X	X	X	X
Engage local sales support/resources/forces	X		X	X	X	X
Keep inventory			X	X	X	X
Employ local administration			X	X	X	X
Local manufacturing					X	X
Re-export to group companies					X	X
FX coverage					X	X
Perform global manufacturing and global supply chain			X	X	X	X
Perform global profit optimisation						X
Perform global tax optimisation						X
Perform global cash optimisation						X

Figure 3.3 International business development model main phases and corresponding economic functions performed.

Turnover) and the remainder sovereign states (measured by their GDPs). In other words, a firm like General Motors, or Wall Mart, or EXXON weighs more than a sovereign state such as Belgium or the Netherlands.

The multinationalisation of a firm characterises a state where a corporation considers the world as its "homeland" and manufactures and sells in multiple nations/countries. But it also means that it manufactures goods in a country and sells those very same goods in the same country where they have been manufactured. In fact, it means that this corporation will manufacture – totally or partially – in whichever country that is best fit (meaning most of the times most cost "effective") and sell in whichever country the market is best suited (meaning most of the time higher selling prices and larger volumes).

The consolidated profit and cash flow level is then globally maximised utilising all possible ways including non-double tax treaties and tax-effective countries (also called off shore centres, IBC (international business centres), tax heavens, etc.).

Typically, the global value-added chain of a product from ore extraction to final sales is broken down into multiple micro steps and segments, all over the world, housed in multiple subsidiaries or joint ventures, always in search of the best profitability/return on investment (ROI).

Multinationalisation is not new, e.g., in the 16th and 17th centuries a British company was producing opium in India and selling it in China. This later resulted in the Chinese rebellion and boxer rebellion.

The same was the case 5000 years ago when copper was extracted in Cyprus (Cyprus gave its name to the metal: copper) and exported to Europe, transformed into weapons or jewels by local craftsmen and re-traded to Middle East and elsewhere.

What is new today is the magnitude of the Multinationalisation process, generally called the second multinationalisation.

This process started mostly post-World War II, and accelerated by the end of the 1980s when Lady Thatcher, the then UK prime minister and Ronald Reagan, the then president of the United States launched an economic revolution aimed at "liberalising" the fluxes of goods and monies across the world and in parallel promoting the reduction of the state's role by shifting to the private interest sectors that used to belong and be controlled by the state: nuclear energy plants, transport systems, education, health, pension schemes, etc.

In parallel, the fall of the USSR coupled with the shift of China towards free market economy with a pace of above 10% growth every year have made the world a gigantic merchant market where anything and everything can be manufactured and sold anywhere and everywhere.

This "creed" was even at the centre of the European Constitution defunct project, replaced now by the "simplified EU treaty" before which the citizens of Holland and France refused to vote for it in referendum.

In summary, almost everything can move freely in today's world from one country to the next, from goods to services to cash, with few regulations; all except human beings, who on the contrary are more and more heavily controlled and restricted (immigration is becoming all the more difficult on the surface of the earth, whilst at the same time the number of refugees is increasing massively).

There is no need to speak of strengths and weaknesses: either you are multinational or you are not.

In terms of controls, however, it all depends if the multinational is operating as an organic global industrial entity or as a financial holding, although split around the world.

In the first case, the focus will be on obtaining a report that gives a comprehensive cross-border view of the economic efficiency of the business processes – a kind of supranational management accounting with all possible zooms in and out, roll backs, aggregations, consolidations, sorts, etc.

Classical reports are multidimensional analyses by countries, products, technologies, etc. However, if a person is in a group's controller position, he/she cannot reasonably be considered to be able to control every single aspect among billions or trillions of daily transactions; therefore, aggregates and synthesis will have to be dealt with most of the time.

In the second case, the focus is clearly more on financial than economic or managerial. In this case, the business must be looked at as so many discrete units, in the way an investment banker or a financial analyst would do, without industrial logic. This obviously means that the reporting stresses less on costs of manufacturing, marketing costs, margins per products, etc., but more on financials, ROCE (Return on Capital Employed), profit per share, dividends paid out, etc.

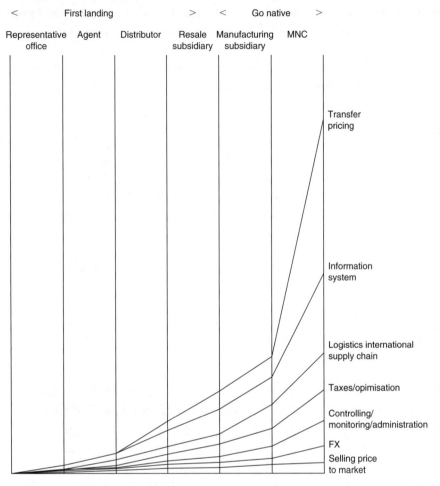

Figure 3.4 Increasing controlling complexity according to internationalisation phases.

So in an MNC the buzzword is information which does not necessarily mean computers systems.

An information system is a system that allows the right information about the right person at the right time, regardless of the mass of data or the technology.

This is why the IS is becoming a critical point in large multinationals (Figures 3.4–3.6).

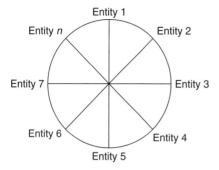

n = number of entities

$$\frac{n(n-1)}{2} = \text{number of communication lines}$$

$$\sim \frac{n^2}{2} = \text{number of communication lines}$$
when n is big

Note: Adding an entity (subsidiaries, project, product line, level etc.) adds the square value of the already existing communication lines.

Figure 3.5 Complexity outgrows the number of entities in the MNC (square function).

Mini case: Nestlé Global Systems

Nestlé, the Swiss-based multinational giant has prospered by leaving a lot of autonomy to its international subsidiaries and has grown organically or by means of acquisitions for over the past 150 years. However, over the past years Nestlé has embarked on a gigantic endeavour in gluing together all its worldwide components onto the same information system to face the challenge of an even more complex and money-oriented world.

Off shoring

It would have been impossible not to mention off shoring, since this form of multinationalisation is very trendy and growing fast.

To start with, there is a matter of definition which is not just of a semantic nature: is a supplier part of the company? Well, at first glance, the technically correct answer would be a direct "no". A supplier is a

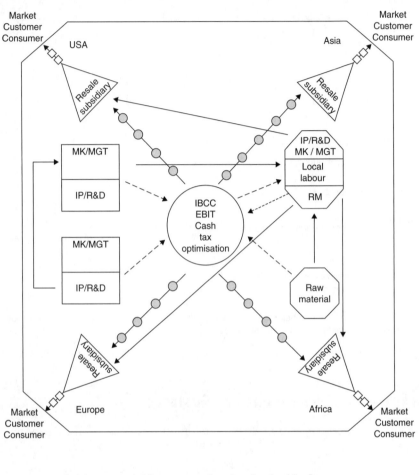

Figure 3.6 Simplified economic, financial and physical flows within an MNC up to 75% of flows are intra group transactions.

distinctively different legal entity – end of the story. End of the story, really? Well, it is also to be recognised that the outsourcing company has in some instances (and more than less) a real control over the subcontractor. This of course proceeds from the concept of "economic" or "social" group, which goes beyond the corporate veil and links within the same perimeter all these distinct legal entities together along the global supply chain.

Needless to say that all employer organisations are fiercely battling against this economic and social group concept, although they are co-signing the work done recently by the UN/ILP as part of the corporate social responsibility of the MNCs.

Off shoring consists in subcontracting part or all of the manufacturing and/or designing to third parties abroad, where the costs are lower.

An interesting project by a team led by Professor Weber from the MIT and published in 2007 (Weber et al., 2007) in the book *How We Compete* revealed the way off shoring was culturally driven, like almost everything in business even if people are not conscious of it. Professor Weber and her team noticed that when the Americans were off shoring in China, in about 90% of cases, they would off shore to an existing Chinese company. On the contrary the Japanese, although physically and geographically closer, would create their own subsidiary off shore in China in 75% of the cases, run by a Japanese management.

Summary

International business development takes many forms depending on the different phase the business is in.

Each phase, from "first landing" to "go native" corresponds to a corporate structure and each structure drives a set of specific controls.

MNCs are large cross-border entities which are not only challenging overeign states and local cultures in terms of economic weight, but are also creating cross-national supply chains. Because MNCs are the main FDI's providers and because 75% of their financial and product/service flows are intra-group, due to their international supply chains, they also re-shape the corporate responsibility definition, thus addressing upfront international corporate governance issues.

However, all MNCs are putting complexity controlling at the centre of their management.

References

Lemaire, J.P. (1998), Stratégies d' internationalisations.
Smith, A. (1776), An Enlightenment in the Nature and the Cause of the Wealth of the Nations.
Weber, S. et al. (2007), How We Compete.

4

Business and their control related issues

4.1 The five fundamental factors that determine, characterise and measure cultural influences

Culture is fundamentally impregnating the way we think, driving every single thing we do. It is all the more comprehensive that we do not *consciously* realise the cultural factors inside us, exactly as we do not naturally realise the air we breathe on a day-to-day basis, yet it's there all the time and keeping us alive. The comparison with air is actually very valid since air has been identified as a living principle in almost all cultures. For the ancient Greeks, the air we breath was intermingled with our soul, the life principle "pneuma", which has given "Anima" in Latin (soul), the "Qi" in Chinese.

Cultures have however been observed from ancient times as different from one's own. The Greek historian Herodotus (484–425 BC) considered the "father of History" had already written his encounters with different people, and their different ways of life.

Over time, cultures have been associated with presupposed characteristics or clichés.

In this vein, Montesquieu, a French philosopher from the period of Enlightenment, in his *Théorie des climats, Ésprit des Lois* categorised cultures according to the climatic conditions (Montesquieu, 1749). He concluded that in warm climates the natives were more prone to be lazy and laid back, with no or limited capacity for initiative. In other words they were born to be "slaves". However Europeans, born in starker climates, were hard workers and prone to make decisions and be consistent with them. They were born leaders or masters.

More recently in the 20th century, anthropologists like Margaret Meads and Claude Levi Strauss, carried out a lot of work in trying to identify the role of culture and nature; particularly in identifying the impact of culture on other civilisations such as the invasion of western culture on the traditional cultures of remote nations and its people.

Only very recently has culture been "scientifically" measured in quantitative terms.

A Dutch engineer, Geert Hofstede (2001), worked in the 1960s as the human resources manager for IBM. He was struck by the fact that the behaviour in business may be very different despite the highly uni-formed set of procedures that IBM imposed worldwide. He elaborated a research methodology that was, and still is, a model in social science, resulting in a questionnaire that he circulated to IBM's 50 000 employ-ees around the world (64 countries) and screened data using multifac-tor analyses. From the analysis, he identified four different factors that would explain more than 70% of the cultural traits. These were as dis-cussed in the following sections.

4.1.1 Power distance

This measures the degree of power inequality distributed in societies. For example, in some societies, such as the French, there is a high power distance, i.e., power is exerted not as a functional element, but as a personal element. In France the boss alone decides, and even out of the office he still remains the boss. At the opposite part of the spectrum, e.g., in Sweden, consensus is the rule. Decisions are made in common and if or when there needs to be a boss it is clearly a functional role, it does not mean that this person is superior to others outside his/her functional role. It is also interesting to note that power distance is almost on a one-to-one direct correlation with the corruption level of a society. France which scores high on the Hofstede power distance scale also scores high on the corruption index which is regularly published by "transparency international" (France ranks 19, close to that of Chile). The relationship to be concluded is that the more the power is personal the higher the possibility of corruption exists.

4.1.2 Individualism versus collectivism

It measures the degree to which individuals are connected to groups within societies. In individualistic societies, individuals are expected to look after themselves, whereas in collectivist societies the group provides a cohesive safety net, e.g. extended families. Note that col-lectivisms have no connection to political systems. Here again, Nordic countries appear to be highly collectivist, whereas interestingly the United States are highly individualistic and southern cultures (espe-cially Latin) tend to be collectivists too.

4.1.3   Masculinity versus its opposite femininity

This has nothing to do with gender distribution of power, but rather in Hofstede's jargon the masculinity is associated with assertive and aggressive traits, where femininity is related to modest and caring values. Another way to state it is hunters versus farmers. Americans are typically "masculine" (hunters) whereas Japanese would be more "feminine" (farmers).

4.1.4   Uncertainty avoidance

This deals with a society's tolerance for uncertainty and ambiguity. Some societies are extremely uncomfortable with the "relative" truth, i.e., countries spun of the Roman Germanic Empire and compensate for ambiguity by complex legal rules or precise engineering. On the contrary, some other societies are comfortable with uncertainty. This is the case for the Anglo-Saxon countries such as the United Kingdom and the United States.

4.1.5   Time horizon

This dimension was added later, after a Hong Kong academic, Michael Bond, found that this dimension was also characterising cultural traits. In simple terms, some cultures have an extended view of time: it does not matter if things happen today or later. This is the case of the Asiatic cultures (called the Confucian dimension), although a timely occurrence is paramount in other societies. This is especially the case of Germany, the United Kingdom and the United States where "time is money".

4.2   The different communication patterns according to cultures and ad hoc reporting styles and contents (explicit, non-explicit, direct or circular, etc.)

Hofstede made a similar breakthrough in cultural science as Copernicus did in physics – a revolution; some other cultural elements are important in cross-cultural management, in particular the way they communicate.

The anthropologist Edward Hall worked a great deal on qualifying the cultures along the lines of communications and actions. Unlike Hofstede, Edward Hall did not quantify the cultures; he established that some cultures had a low context and other a high context in terms of communications (Hall, 1959).

Low context means that very few elements are connected to the context in the communication. Everything is out of context and made explicit. Whereas a high context culture entails the exact opposite of communication: almost everything is connected to the context, and implicit. It means there is a need to read between the lines, and a lot of communication is non-verbal. On an average, the non-verbal communication covers 70% of the context of a communication. In case of high context it will be a lot more. For example, the French tend to have a high context culture. Things are not made explicit and one must read between the lines. Furthermore, body language speaks louder than the words. On the contrary, Americans are low context. In a contract, e.g., everything would be stated, even the obvious, for purpose of clarity.

Therefore, one can easily imagine the difficulty in business negotiations or in reporting between those two cultures.

Hall also distinguished between being polychronic and monochronic. This means that in some cultures it is common to do several things at once (mostly in Latin, and Arabic cultures), whereas in other cultures things are executed in sequence one after the other: in a typical Germanic or American way. Of course the polychronic might not be on time in everything they do, and will invariably appear towards the monochronic as negligent or disorganised in a given situation where they would see themselves as highly efficient as juggling several things at the same time. Conversely, monochronic would appear as "limited" and "rigid" to polychronics since they do not deliver much and do it at a slow pace (one thing at a time), thus relatively inefficient. This is typical in the story of a German engineer who is sent to a plant in south of Spain to solve an "emergency" on a production line. The German tends to methodically take one problem after the other, exasperating the Spaniards who expected a lot to be achieved at once in all directions. If this is then coupled with the Spanish high context and the Germanic low context styles, immediately an explosive situation occurs, albeit all parties are doing their very best to sort out the same issue – in just culturally opposite ways.

Richard Lewis, who wrote *When Cultures Collide* (Lewis, 2005), insists on speech style, oscillating according to cultures between a straight and minimal communication: like the Finnish, or on the contrary a circular type of communication like the South Americans or the Arabs, where the main point is actually never mentioned but progressively worked towards after different circles/parabolas, in an allusive long winded way.

This kind of information is important to know, and respect, when, e.g., working on a reporting exercise. In this case if there is a group controller on the receiving end who is a Swedish or a Finnish, and on the emitting end there is a middle eastern, it can be hypothesised that on the one hand a fact-only report, minimal in size and full of numbers would be expected, whereas on the other hand, the report would provide a lot of useful information on the subject but also contextual, which may be worded in an allusive or parabolic way, which would be disregarded or ignored by the receiver, even if it contained vital inputs. The fact that they may both use the same ERP or information software makes no difference to this information depletion.

Lewis in his book *When Cultures Collide*, actually takes a very similar approach to the one taken by Hall (cf supra), but looking at the communication format, Hall observed that some cultures are fact- and figures-oriented (the Anglo-Saxons, the Germans) and others are process-oriented (the Arabs, the Latins, etc.).

For Hall, people and process cultures give utmost importance to the way things are done, the style and what they are purported for. They will also give a very important weight to the personal side.

Mini case: Khaled, John and conflict of interests

In other words one could say, "I do business with Khaled firstly because I know him, I know his family to whom I am related, I know how he works, he is efficient and dependable, I can trust him, my company's interests are in good hands". Whether Khaled works for company ABC or XYZ is of a secondary importance, almost insignificant.

It can immediately be seen that the typically Western-originated concept of arm's length is to some extent culturally antagonist to this. In the Anglo-Saxon culture, a person would firstly work with company ABC, because ABC was screened and selected over firms XYZ and EFG after an independent five-tier selection process based on an open auction/bidding process. Now if John, a college mate and brother-in-law to the person happens to work for company ABC as the lead person in that deal, it suddenly becomes a major problem. In the Anglo-Saxon culture it is considered that there is a major conflict of interest, resulting in company ABC being disqualified, or as a solution John and/or the person concerned being assigned another project. Should this information not be reported upfront in the United States or in a US-controlled company, there is a procedure under the Sarbanes–Oxley rule that insists that any third party may denounce a presumed conflict of interest of a colleague, protected by anonymity and a telephone line, whilst triggering an in-depth enquiry about the person or individual.

The people- and process-oriented culture is currently the dominant culture in the world. It covers approximately 92% of the world population today including southern Europe, the Mediterranean countries, the whole of Africa, Near East and Middle East, Central Asia, partially Russia, and the vast majority of the ex-USSR republics, and populated countries/regions such as India and Asia and the Pacific countries.

In contrast, management models, which are vastly (in the majority as 98% of global management literature) produced in North America and written in English, were initially designed and engineered in cultural areas representing less than 8% of the world population, before they became disseminated worldwide.

Mini case: The "Guanxhi" factor in China

The relationship factor is paramount in the social organisation, particularly in China. Not only are the people and process important as a cultural trait, but also in doing business efficiently. What is it all about? As all societies are people-oriented, the people known to a person constitute a web of relationships – a network. This is a living network that is fed by the efforts given to it. In other words, if Chang is in my network and Tang is not, I shall more likely connect with Chang when I want to buy something. Likewise I may ask Chang to do me a favour, such as an introduction to a friend of his from part of his network in New York, who would be able to give me insight into the US market for my products and eventually market them for me acting as my distributor. This web of networking is called "guanxhi". The more "guanxhi" you have the more important and respected you become. "Guanxhi" is not something static; it is made to be "returned". In other words, when you used the "guanxhi" of somebody you are expected to "return" the "guanxhi" some day. It must be remembered that the time horizon for an Asian is quasi-infinite, thus for you or your relatives (the extended family culture is dominant in China).

At this stage it is important to understand that this is not only perfectly correct for the Chinese, but it is their normal and traditional way of doing things. This view by Westerners, not aware of the cultural differences and full of the "facts and figures" of their own culture, would probably appear close to corruption.

Mini case: The French Grandes Écoles and Grands Corps Network

In France, 95% of the CAC 40 (equivalent to Dow Jones or FT 500) top business leaders, government ministers, high-ranking civil servants come from a handful of "Grandes Écoles" which are a kind of selective "elite" schools. The French social scientist Bourdeux in many instances characterised this "closed" network as the Noblesse d'État, today's replacement for monarchy and nobility. Furthermore coming from the École Nationale de l'Administration (ENA) or Polytechnique (X) in France is a fast track to power, privilege, prosperity, lifelong employment and quasi-immunity (Grand Corps d'État).

4.2.1   And the "cyber Guanxhi" coming from the West

Although people and process are not culturally an Anglo-Saxon cultural trait, it is interesting to see that a new "wave" of cyber networking tools, such as "Face Books", emanating from the Anglo-Saxon sphere is rapidly expanding – the objective being to mimic a cyber guanxhi.

4.3   The different business organisations and their relative fit or misfits with main business cultures (why matrix is sometimes a mess, why flat organisation are not always working, etc.)

Some cultures tend to naturally drive some organisation forms. For example, the cultures where a high power distance exists drives towards a highly hierarchical form of society. Think of the countries where the Power Distance Index (PDI) is high according to Hofstede (*Cultures consequences 2001*, Second Edition, Sage Publications). These are Guatemala (95), Panama (95), Mexico (81) and Venezuela (81). All these Amerindian nations were used to having an extremely hierarchical society ruling for as long as a millennium (the Olmecs, the Toltecs, the Mayas and the Aztecs), where the absolute power was held by a group of individuals enjoying a godly status. When the "conquistadors" invaded them they added even more hierarchy and absolute power, reinforcing the highly hierarchical structure. No wonder the power distance is culturally high today.

Arab countries also tend to have a high power index (80), along with Indonesia (78), India (77), Africa (77) and China – Hong Kong (68).

In Europe, France stands out with the highest score, 68 (Italy, 50;, Great Britain, 35 and Denmark, only 18).

In these countries the cultural business organisational model is the pyramid. Undoubtedly it is the model that perfectly fits the culture.

In countries with a low PDI, such as Great Britain (35), Switzerland (34), Finland (33), Norway (31), Sweden (31) and Denmark (18), the "flat" organisation is the perfect match to the culture.

Mini case: The "matrix" organisation a quasi-universal cultural "misfit"

The matrix organisation is an artificial form of organisation that emerged close to the end of the 1960s and beginning of the 1970s under the drive of a very famous US-based management consulting firm. The United States was a medium-range country in terms of PDI (40) and was enjoying a formidable foreign trade expansion via the MNCs. There soon came a point where traditional functional organisations were also centralised from the United States. In other words, domestically the business organisation was, as they learned from Mr. Taylor, a self-made engineer at Ford and Mr. Sloane a general manager at General Motors (GM), segmented and specialised by the diverse functions they had to perform. In other words, there were the sales- and production function, which were the two basic business processes, and then the finance and administrative- and the R&D function, which were basic support functions. But when it came to monitor and control foreign subsidiary in Africa, or Europe, or Latin America, it just was too far to be centrally and functionally controlled from Minnesota or Chicago or New York. For other reasons, it was unthinkable to let these foreign subsidiaries have full autonomy, although the US-educated native speaking bosses managed them. Coupled with this control challenge came another business challenge: the business fashion was "diversification" and "conglomeratisation". Again another very famous East Coast–originated advisory firm devised and proved a bright concept that diversification was the ultimate business model. Business diversification allowed to safeguard against different business cycles that would not occur at the same time, and geographical diversification would give the possibility to take advantage of different business opportunities and self-insure against foreign exchange and economic risks. This is how the seed of the matrix was planted: the organisation would be two-dimensional (and soon multi-): on one dimension you would find the traditional business functions (sales, production, finance, R&D) and on the other the geographies. In other words, a sales manager in France would have two bosses to obey or satisfy: the sales director back in the United States and the local subsidiary managing director. This kind of organisational chimera does not of course fit in with the culturally high PDI countries. In those cultures it is unconceivable to have two bosses. The loyalty is either towards the functional boss or the local managing director. In cases of conflicting directives it is not, as clearly argued by the US consulting firm, a stabilising factor for enhanced efficiency, on the contrary it is the perfect vehicle for paralysis, and a clear invitation to become a traitor, plotting, conspiring and playing "politics". Ultimately, the economic global performance becomes inferior and the working climate deteriorates. For low PDI countries, the matrix does not work either. Low PDI countries have to decide (almost everything) unanimously. The boss only fulfils a "referee" or senior advisory function, a "primus inter pares", not at all a "pater familias" role. A matrix organisation does not make any sense to them either since it introduces the conflict has a structural to decision making.

Mini case: Who is the boss in France?

A few years ago the French subsidiary's strategic plan of a large chemical corporation commenced by stating in a strengths, weaknesses, opportunities, threats (SWOT) analysis, where their main challenge was – who is the boss?

That particular year was special as a line of pharmaceutical products, invented and manufactured in the United States were to be imported and sold in France. Needles to say that the US pharmaceuticals (anaesthetics) had successfully passed all the French regulatory tests and controls before being introduced into the French market. However, the French law in those days insisted that the moment a company started selling pharmaceuticals, its CEO had to be a qualified pharmacist (PhD and chartered pharmacist). This immediately resulted in the divisional manager of the pharmaceutical products division, who had the right qualifications, becoming the CEO of the whole subsidiary (legal entity) in France; thus heading all the other divisional heads, including the current subsidiary managing director who happened to be the country manager. The matrix organisation was just not working. This case also poses the problem of legal entity bosses and thus carries heavy legal responsibility vis à vis third parties in a given country, whether just "steered" from the "matrix" above them and doing things in order that may be heavily conflicting with what their local duties may be.

Mini case: Flat organisations do not work in Brazil

A "flat organisation" is another management fashion that advocates that organisations must be "flattened", i.e., hierarchical levels should be cut down to a maximum of three for costs squeezing reasons (even if this might not be present in this fashion). Heated debates took place to know whether it should be three levels including the top one, that of the CEO, meaning just two for any organisation be it 200 employees or 200 000 employees or without the CEO, leaving three "full" levels for 199 employees to 199 999 employees.

Whilst advising a large Swedish multinational (remember Sweden has one of the lowest PDI and is highly "feminine" according to the Hofstede distribution) which had embarked into this venture, help for the Brazilian subsidiary was needed (5 industrial plants, 17 000 employees) which seemed to be "slow" to adjust to the three-level new era. After investigating the local company it became obvious that the local organisation was perfectly consistent with the local culture, i.e., high PDI, including the business- and plant set-ups. More specifically there were up to eight layers of hierarchy with three to four layers of "gerantes" formed of supervisors to middle managers. These "gerantes" far from being useless layers, representing idle costs, were in fact very active DNA components of the living organisations. They were bosses of small, human size clusters, where problems were solved as and when they occurred and workers were trained and guided permanently. In other words, not only were they useful, but were also in harmony with the local culture, and participating in the overall performance of the company; the Brazilian operations being one of the best performers in the world.

Finally, it was decided to leave things as they were and not to brutally "export" the flat organisation model that was not culturally compatible and was thus leading to inferior performance.

4.4 The different cultural attitudes towards control and the relative (in)adequacy of the most common reporting systems

The word "control" by itself does not have the same meaning in different languages.

Languages are deep-rooted in a culture and vice versa. All linguists from Chomsky to Hagège agree on this. It is very common that words existing in one given language just do not exist in another language, or that their meaning may be slightly or deeply altered.

Mini case: The Inuits and the white colour(s)

The Inuits are people who live near the North Pole. It is an almost closed society that had to adapt to survive under such difficult natural conditions. They are constantly surrounded with snow and ice – an all white world. However, depending on the seasons and the moment in the day, or on the weather conditions, the white colour varies – the ice and snow may be hard, fresh, soft, melting, powder, damp, dry, etc., . And these variations in the white colour, reflect that variations in their environment are of utmost importance to their survival, as they have learned over millennia. The result is that the Inuits have over 17 distinct words for "white", depending of what kind of white they are speaking about. We have only one "white." Therefore, when we say "white" it is impossible to translate this correctly into the Inuit language. Conversely, we invariably translate all their words into one – simply white because the concept of different white does not exist at 40º latitude. Although it is scientifically evident, most of the time it is not clearly acknowledged or known that a language is dependent on the culture from which it originated, and a concept is intrinsically dependent on a language from which it has been formulated.

Now moving to the accounting scene it can be seen in the following that within Europe the accounting cultures are profoundly different, if not antagonistic (Figure 4.1).

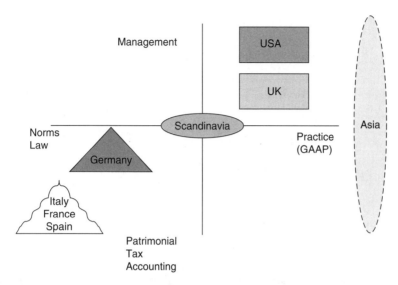

Figure 4.1 Controlling cultural orientations.

In France, Spain and Italy, e.g., the accounting language serves the purpose of establishing and maintaining a communication with the legal authorities (not the business community) in both its purpose: assessing the taxes immediately owed to the state and one's properties (what actually belongs to a person).

As a result accounting is neither management- nor business process–oriented. Instead the taxes and the most important of all in terms of tax influx for the state: the value-added tax (which can be up to 60–70% of the fiscal influx paid into the state budget) are at the centre of the profit and loss statement (Figure 4.2).

Taking this consideration one step further, the way transactions are accounted (substance) for are commanded by the structure where every single transaction is characterised by law ("plan comptable" in France) in all its infinite detail, and governed by the chart of accounts. Every account is pre-set by law in its coding and numbering. There are neither industry specifics nor flexibility by company type. This is done to facilitate the standardised tax audit and also to serve the national economic statistics ("Comptabilité Nationale" in France) where the GDP is obtained by (almost) simply adding up the respective companies' value-added lines. As a funny example, imagine a company such as a call centre. Last

Latin–P&L Legal/property/angle	Anglo-Saxon–P&L Managerial/Business Process/Practice angle
• Revenues • Inventory variation • Purchase • Outsourced services • ADDED VALUE • Personnel charges • Depreciation • Financial charges • Profit • Taxes	• Sales • Cost of manufacture • R&D • Distribution cost • Sales and Marketing • Administration cost • PROFIT/EBIT • Financial cost • Taxes

Figure 4.2 Cultures drive P&L structures.

year this company decided to outsource their workforce. If reporting under the French Law standards, it would have to record its entire workforce under "services extérieurs", thus not creating any "value added". If this same company pursues the same business, logic decides to lease its entire telecom equipment. It would record just zero under fixed assets.

The very same company under US GAAPs would record its personnel under cost of sales (regardless of whether they are temporary staff or are salaried employees with the company), thus giving a solid understanding of the gross margin formation. Conversely a return on capital employed (ROCE) will be made meaningful.

If the management team now changes its views and decides to in-source its workforce the following year and purchases its leased assets, all things being otherwise equal, no change under UK and US GAAPs would result in massive change in the Latin-based accounting system (France, etc.).

Furthermore, in the Latin world only those things that actually belong to the company are recorded in the balance sheet as assets. A fundamental piece of machinery that is not owned but leased instead will not appear on the balance sheet.

In the Anglo-Saxon culture, however, accounting is meant to help management make business decisions and shareholders assess how the company is performing to allow cross-company/industry benchmarking.

This profound cultural imprint is pivotal to the construction of the US or UK profit and loss in that the P&L lines are organised to reflect business key processes: sales, cost of sales/manufacture, selling and marketing, administration, finance cost, etc

This is informative to management in the relative cost to sales, as it is to a shareholder who can compare/benchmark with other companies operating in the same industry.

The balance sheet also allows meaningful key ratios to be obtained like ROI (return on investment) or ROCE (return on capital employed) by considering a piece of equipment as an asset used in the process of generating profit regardless of its mode of acquisition/financing, be it leased or owned; thus allowing shareholder intra-industry and general performance comparisons.

It can be clearly seen at this point that the two main (accounting) languages are modelled by fundamentally different views, i.e., on how relationships with management, the business community, shareholders and the state should be conducted. These cultural differences are expressed through different languages which are perfect in depicting certain realities (in relation to the state and the law in France/Latin countries) and very clumsy in others (business processes efficiency in France/Latin Countries) because they are simply not relevant in the said culture.

The question that can then be asked is: How to standardise the two languages into one "uniform" European language?

This question is not new for linguists. It is a recurrent theme of language appropriation and domination. Basically, the most efficient scenario over time has been the domination of one language over the other, thus reducing diversity and ambiguity to increase accuracy and efficiency.

For example, Greek was the universal language in the whole of the Mediterranean world during the time of Christ and the centuries that followed. It supplanted Latin although this was the official language of the Empire, because it was deep-rooted for a longer time and more efficient in business. The same applied to the Anglo-Saxon dialects which eventually dominated the Celtic language in Britain when the Angles and the Saxons, fleeing the Barbarians, invaded Britain.

Thus, the most frequent case for linguists is that the language follows the dominance, be it economic or military or intellectual. Composed languages of mixed influences such as pidgins never make to the status of a real language and never last long.

Artificial languages do exist, the most known is Esperanto, created slightly more than a century ago. Esperanto was a fantastic artificial language. It was simple to read, write and learn. Why did it never become an official language? Despite its intrinsic qualities that were fantastic it was simply lacking an underlying culture (and economic power) from which to root.

In the case of IFRS (International Financial Reporting System), the European Union (EU) could not favour any language from the Latin-/ Continental-based, over the Anglo-Saxon culture and conversely could not afford monetarily and politically, to create an artificial accounting and reporting language from scratch.

Since EU is by its very construction highly federative, it did what it was genetically encoded to do: "assemble" the two existing languages in a "federative" way.

Given that there is a fundamental antagonism between the Anglo-Saxon and Latin concept, the EU decided, via the IASB, to circumvent the issue by developing a "wrap up" mechanism aimed at using the minimal common denominator between two opposite sets of cultures, and thus languages. In practice this has given birth to the hybrid philosophy where only the consolidated entities would speak "IFRS", the "composite language" using the "principles" – the phonemes – as meta-language, not the basic entities where the real business is performed which will still keep their "dialect"/local books. The good reason behind this is that it would otherwise deprive the local states in Continental Europe of an easy access to tax controls (being so culturally driven that tax books and management accounts are just a single set of books), which are far from being standardised in EU.

From a linguistic point of view, the IFRS can be compared to a regression where an advanced alphabetical language (using few – 26 – precise signs/letters combined together to form sounds (phonemes) which in turn determine related objects/concepts) is turned back into a phonemic anguage where macro elements (the composite categories) designate pre-identified patterns. This naturally results in a more clumsy language where, far from having 17 words for white there might only be three colours – black, white or grey, with 85% of the objects being "named" by the word "grey", by default of requested "precision level".

4.5 Planning, budgeting and other "future telling" dimensions: their relative (non)importance in different cultural areas. The specific cases of china and India. The notion of time and their related controlling points: target settings, plans, return on investments, pay back period versus different cultures vis à vis time: linear, circular, finite, infinite, recurring etc.

Time is a key parameter of business. It is the alpha and the omega of any investment evaluation, be it measured in terms of payback period, or discounted cash flows, IRRs or company valuations.

Time is also the backbone of accounting: it is the base rock in the "historical" accounting principle – a fundamental element in accounting – in depreciation calculations in impairment tests, cut-offs, etc.

However, time is also fundamental to any culture. In some cultures, time is scarce and has a monetary value. Time is linear and always moves in the same direction. In the cultures where time is linear, people are most of the time monochronic.

The nations where this type of culture of time broadly exists are: western Europe and Northern America, i.e., 8% of the world population.

For 92% of the world, time is not sequential, non-linear, but abundant and circular. In these regions people are most of the time polychronic.

Two main factors explain this distribution:

Religious belief: In the West, the basic principle of Christianity is that whatever good or bad a person has been in this life will drive him or her to either heaven or hell (with a vast array of nuances of course). The point is that the person has only one life to live, one chance "to make it" and therefore time is scarce, sequential and linear and precious. In other parts of the world, Asia, India, and to some extent Africa and the Pacific Rim, the dominant religious belief (with lots of variation according to each specific) is in having several lives to live. According to how good or bad a person has "performed" in this life will define the next life and so on until "perfection". No time limit, no "one shot" concept here: time is not important per se, time is not scarce, and time is abundant. The person has plenty of time to achieve what he or she is here to do; the important point is continuous improvement in the different incarnations, leaving the possibility to even restart all over again.

The proximity to nature: Some people are disconnected totally from nature: most of the population in Western societies (western Europe, North America) is "urban" ranging from 85% to 97%.

In contrast, the urban population ranges from 15 % to 30% in Africa, South Asia, India, China, – although the urbanisation rate is accelerating and probably in 2050, most of the megapolis will be located in Asia and Africa; the bigger picture is that they still remain rural population-based regions.

It means that the connection with nature was and is still very profound. It is a matter of fact that nature is cyclical by "nature" – at least as seen from the human perception, seasons do come back at regular intervals, light and darkness do come back at regular intervals, fundamental biological rhythms are cyclical, etc. Time is therefore seen as cyclic in nature.

This fundamental perception difference of time and nature according to cultures is the cause of many misunderstandings, misconceptions and even clashes in business.

Mini case: The thousand lotus business plan versus the thousand cells spreadsheet

The sun was setting on the Towers of Notre Dame Cathedral in Paris (France), and so were the last days of the second millennium. I was in a posh apartment located at the top of an ancient building on the Ile de la Cité in the historical heart of Paris-named Lutecia by the Romans, which started off as a small village 2000 years ago. A loop was closing.

A new era was beginning with this Asia project ahead of us. The discussion had been going on for more than a year, and we were here to come to a conclusion. I was advising the chairman of the board and owner of a very well-known French cosmetics laboratory on his expansion plan in China. We were having a round of negotiations with a group of investors from China with whom we wanted to form a joint venture to break into and capture a fair share of the Chinese market.

Without going into the technical details of the deal, selling these luxury cosmetics in Europe as part of qualified "soins" merchandised through "beauty clinics" and through spas in the United States was the key marketing vehicle.

Our joint venture Chinese investors were here in Paris, in the owner's apartment domineering the river Seine, a hundred metres from the Notre Dame Cathedral. They had come all the way from Shanghai and Honk Kong, specifically to present the business plan. They had developed the business plan as they were to be the local operators and co-investors in the "beauty clinics", whilst the French cosmetics company was providing the trademark as well as the products for the high end, and the IP/licensees for the medium-range cosmetics. They had been quite secretive about the business plan and did not want to send anything via the Internet, as they preferred to present it "live". And this was today.

The youngest member, opened his leather attaché case and pulled out a thin red file covered with a single Chinese character.

He opened the file that had one page of quality paper with a couple of Chinese signs, and beside this on a separate page the English translation. It read "our joint business plan is to build one thousand lotus flowers together".

And that was the end of the story.

The French cosmetics firm owner was embarrassed; he had just invested in 30 spas in the United States a few months ago and he was expecting more or less a similar presentation: a thousands lotus spreadsheets with figures, drawings, valuations, DFC's market shares, etc. Instead he was getting a promise – 1000 lotus flowers. Of course each lotus was representing a beauty clinic.

After a moment of silence, the French gentleman asked in surprise: But what is the time line? How are you going to get precisely to the 1000th – and why 1000?

The answer he got from the most senior Chinese investor came straight and clear: 1000 is symbolic; it means plenty and prosperity and so is the lotus. In reality it could have just been any number. And he continued explaining that the number is not in itself important. What is important is to get the first "beauty clinic" working, and working perfectly. Then it will expand. The country is big, the size is there and they have the experience (they had other pharmaceutical businesses working extremely well).

The very idea of putting minute detailed plans and tight time frames for something that did not even exist yet was absolutely alien to our Chinese partners. They just could not see the point.

Finally, they reached an agreement and today, 7 years later, they have exceeded the initial "business plan" of 1000 beauty clinics. In China, do it the Chinese way could be the answer to the story.

4.5.1 Can Westerners really tell and plan the future better?

The Western culture, has always tried to plan and control the future. With powerful computing support and communication capabilities boxed in ever-smaller volumes, today the temptation to forecast the future is very high. This corresponds to the need in cultures with a relative high degree of uncertainty avoidance.

But what is it in reality?

Mini case: Forecasting versus Fortune telling: MBA versus Psychic reader?

Forecasting is a temptation that is actually very ancient in the sense of reading and thus mastering the future; as ancient as the emergence of mankind itself.

This attitude is of course driven by the fact that men are not so pleased with their present "miserable" intrinsic condition but, for most of them, aspire to rival with deities and gods in having the vision of the future; thus a grip on their destiny.

The person, who has or claims to have this capacity to read and shape the future, has always enjoyed a special status in human society, much praised in power games.

Forecasting capabilities, mostly, were connected with religion and religious rituals, among other things, to keep the ordinary man away from this exclusive art/gift/relationship. That was the time of the shaman, future tellers, mages, etc.

4.5.2 From the renaissance period the emerging scientific paradigm gradually dominated the market share of the future telling market over and above the traditional magic "art/gift" paradigm

During the Renaissance and the century of Enlightenment, statesmen and kings used divination before doing anything important, be it in the ancient Near East (Mesopotamia) as long ago as 3500 BC to read lambs livers, or to read Joseph's dreams advising Ramses II about the seven fat cows and the seven skinny cows, or the famous pithy in Delphi advising both the two contending superpowers of those days: Alexander the Great of Greece and Darius of Persia. From the 16th century, emerging organised science began to make headway into divination and started to take its fair share of social power vis-à-vis the greats of this world, in establishing what is still today the paradigm of "hard" sciences: predictability and reproducibility. This is known as the Copernican revolution.

The best example of this attitude in conquering the dominant forecasting market share versus magic divination certainly shows in the theories of Isaac Newton. Here it looks at the world as if it was exclusively governed by mechanical rules where a given cause would derive a predictable effect on the grounds of a "sound mechanical" cause to effect model (rule of physics or mathematical theorem). Interestingly, Isaac was one of the most advanced "alchemist" of his time but at the same time he believed personally in the intrinsic magical nature of the world. To an extent the same applied to Ana of Lovelace, the famous British mathematician (whose name has been used to name a very powerful programming language: ANA). It is said that the contents of her discoveries were dictated to her by her dead father's spirit, the late Lord Byron.

This positive scientific forecasting model went well for about 400 centuries where the same causes would produce the same effects, provided the mechanical model was right. This "scientific" model heavily influenced the emerging economist's theories. One excellent example is probably the Malthus concept where natural resources and human population are bound to follow pre-determined mathematical models (arithmetical progression and geometrical progression) without any disruption or crossover.

This paradigm is known as deterministic, even the probabilistic models were in essence of a deterministic approach (according to well-established rules, a cause would produce well-determined effects).

4.5.3   Cracks in the ceiling appeared at the turn of the 19th century

However, at the turn of the 19th century some cracks started to appear in the deterministic paradigm ceiling under the reflections of a handful of bright and unconventional thinkers who introduced the idea that causes and effects might be inter-linked, even interacting (Goedel and the incompleteness theorem, Einstein: time and space), and that causes might follow the effect (de Brogli and Poincarré), and that propositions might be at the same time right and wrong (Max Planck and Gallois).

Later in the 20th century, at the beginning of the 1970s, it became clear that most of the natural phenomena, including social phenomena to which economics and management belong, were of a "chaotic" nature meaning that causes interact with effects. This was particularly exemplified by Lorentz, a meteorologist researcher, who focused on the, now very well-known "butterfly effect". This is where a butterfly waving its wings in Hong Kong could provoke a storm in New York, thus stressing the sensitivity to initial conditions as well as unpredictability.

Another aspect of this "chaotic" versus deterministic aspect has been characterised by the researches of Mandelbrot, a researcher at IBM, establishing the "fractals", where patterns would replicate regardless of the scale of observation (the shape of a coastline is the same as that of the leaves of the trees planted along this coastlines etc).

In scientific terms, this new paradigm is known as non-linear equations.

4.5.4 In terms of business forecasting however we still live with the 16th century deterministic paradigm

Basically economic and management forecasting models are built on the old order linear/deterministic models unlike the other sciences which have come to terms with chaotic or non-linear concepts that govern our world, still assuming that a given set of causes will necessarily produce the same set of effects. Suffice to take a look at stock fluctuations and M&A activities: as soon as the rumour or information is given that a company is about to acquire its international competitor, the shares tend to soar, whereas it should be the contrary – from a pure deterministic/rational point of view since all analyses show that 75% of international M&A turn to be fiascos after 5 years.

Shares prices are soaring because stock holders (or better said stock flippers) speculate that the magical post of M&A "rationalisation" benefits or enhanced consolidated profits (being the effect) will pay back much more than the uplifted share price (the cause), in that the increased share price should reflect an actually achieved and delivered financial performance and come after the fact. This simple example is a case where the effect precedes the cause, thus forming a typical non-linear/chaotic model that is impossible to forecast with deterministic models; however, sophisticated they may be, they are just not appropriate, as much as it would not be appropriate to use the 16th century science to explain quantum physics.

Thus we are faced with a paradox in economic and management forecasting today, where we have very powerful and sophisticated tools (mainly computers, calculators, spreadsheets and telecommunications) but still face a near-vacuum in terms of forecasting concepts.

Mini case: Global M&A in the Transit Industry in 2005

So far all this may look a bit theoretical, thus let us introduce a practical example that occurred in the course of an international business and management consulting practice. The board of directors of two major global transit companies decided to engage in a global merger of their businesses and they asked for support in this complex international project.

One of the most important part of the exercise was to make a valuation of both the business corporations. Naturally the investment bankers and accountants started and applied the very classical methods and variants revolving around the discounted cash flows of the next 3–5 years to define what would be the terminal value of the (combined) businesses. For those who are less familiar with the technicalities, the terminal value of a business is based on the sum (discounted by a combination of factors) of the future infinite cash flows of the business. Yes, believe it or not, you read it correctly: infinite cash flows.

When both respective business plans for future cash flows were looked into with the teams from both sides, it was found that up to 60% of the revenues (and same for cash flows) were "to be found projects". Because of the very nature of their activities (large transit projects worldwide) cash flows from projects were more or less well identified for the next year and the following year. In other words, the majority of the anticipated cash flow as of the third year was blue sky input.

Moving one notch further, to years 4 and 5, 70–85% were "blue sky/to be found" inputs apart from recurrent maintenance contract, which were not due for renewal in that period.

There is nothing wrong in particular with these two corporations as they are top tier global-listed players in their industry, and their accounting and controlling are meticulously maintained. The problem is not with the companies but with the concept: on the one hand the economic theory calls for a series of infinite cash flows (terminal value) and on the other hand, after year 2, 70–80% of the data is totally guessed (to be found projects/blue sky projects).

This is simply amazing. But if one looks at different industries, it is most probably the same case, to a greater or lesser extent.

Thus, the teams and we went one step further and tried to gauge the capacity for the two firms to deliver their overall corporate cash flow forecasts over the past years. In both cases, this exercise was made difficult because both firms were engaged in non-linear activities over the past years (acquisitions, divestments, turnarounds etc.), actually a troubled history, but again this is the case for a large proportion of firms today, which have gone through many restructuring and M&As over the past 10 years, making troubled records and history.

We decided, therefore to track back 3 years as to what the realisation rate of the forecast was on a project-by-project basis,

The result was amazing here too: the forecast, in terms of project acquisitions (which is the easiest, as gauging the future forecast cash flows is even tougher) was 32% for one firm and 38% for the other.

This means that, on an average the project acquisition (being the master forecast from which all the rest, revenue and cash flow derive) was consistently wrong two times out of three. This is rather interesting, considering that a financial valuation model requires precision on infinite cash flows.

Even more interesting was another finding made through this exercise: if only one project out of three that were forecasted was actually acquired, one to two other projects actually acquired, although not forecasted at all, were against all odds, thus creating some kind of balance.

This case exemplifies exactly the difference between a linear, mechanistic, deterministic paradigm and a turbulent chaotic environment.

4.5.5 Culture is the brake to forecasting and to adapt to turbulent times

This case shows clearly that the forecasting mechanisms, regardless of how brutal the computing force used, or how micro detailed they may be, are not satisfactory per se, since they rely on linear deterministic logic, which we now know, cannot represent the social and economic world. However, the case has showed us that, the sort of compensating mechanism where 2 out of 3 forecasted projects never come true in a 1–3 year horizon, whereas 1 to 2 projects, never taught of, do "pop up", is only attributable to the management culture and attitude. In this case a wining culture based on creativity and lateral thinking, a sort of "can do attitude", which is not easily modelled in spreadsheet made it possible.

This prompts the question: What is the value of the formal forecasting exercise in a corporation, especially in turbulent times like the one we currently experience?

From a purely factual point of view, one must acknowledge that the output (accuracy predictability) over the past 30 years is constantly and consistently disappointing, where things started to get less linear subsequent to the first oil crisis in 1974. Suffice to ask oneself: Who forecasted the upcoming of the personal computer? Not even IBM the super king at the time, whose CEO dared to declare publicly in the early 1980s that a PC had no place in the private household. IBM nearly died from this. More recently, who would have forecasted that the film giant Kodak would go ailing in no time, having failed to understand the market shift from silver to digital. Only a few years ago who would have dared guessed that the "Kaiser" Daimler Group, would miserably fall flat on its face during the mega merger with Chrysler, and conversely, Toyota and Nissan would become the stars of the automotive business to the extent that Toyota has become the number one manufacturer in the world as well as becoming the number two automotive manufacturer on US soil where it employs more people than IBM, Dell and Chrysler put together.

Interestingly enough, this question of scientific predictability in economics and management sciences has always attracted very famous minds. A very interesting experience to remember of the mid-eighties is the very highly publicised attempt to identify what was the gene of success from an immense array of companies data and sophisticated computer-aided analyses.

Tom Peters, published his findings in the book *In Search of Excellence*, which became a global bestseller in no time, filling up the shelves of both airport bookshops and academic libraries (Peters and Waterman, 1982).

Tom Peters then identified 10 corporations that were considered to be global role models for those CEOs who embarked on the quest of enduring top-tier performance.

The irony is that 10 years later, 9 out of 10 of these corporations were bankrupt , and the 10th one that escaped bankruptcy, but almost wounded to death, was IBM.

Tom Peters' model failed to predict the future not because it lacked sophisticated maths, or huge computing power, or educated manpower; it was just that the underlying paradigm was wrong: economic phenomena are not of a linear nature, they are of a chaotic/fractal nature and causes are mixed with effects. Likewise the end pattern is overwhelmingly influenced by the nano differences in initial conditions (the butterfly effect), and looking in the rear mirror at the straight easy motorway from the 1950s to 1980s does not particularly prepare one for the winding roller coaster ahead: the 21st century.

However, the Western culture is almost entirely built on deterministic, hierarchical, cause to effect paradigm. This pattern prevails everywhere in classical Western corporations.

4.5.6 Does this mean that forecasting is a waste of effort?

This would be a wrong conclusion.

Forecasting the way we have been doing it over the past 30 years is certainly a waste of time, energy and effort. Even the very advocated rolling forecasts at present are no better. Why? Because they tend to improve the predication accuracy by diminishing the time horizon, in the same way as it would be more reliable to forecast tomorrow's weather than next month's. However, given the circumstances and the vast amount of data to collect, refresh, scrutinise, assess, process, evaluate and synthesise, it turns out that a company's lead time to produce a next day's weather forecast is more likely to be 3 days, with a 30–40% hit rate. See the catch? Furthermore, the cost of running a rolling forecast is horrendous because it needs a permanent army of staff/controllers as well as representing a strong distraction to operational staff, keeping them away from real customers whilst feeding spreadsheet and attending internal presentations.

4.6 Delegation of authority (budgets, projects, subsidiaries) versus cultures (collective/shared authority)

The delegation of authority is fundamental in business controlling. In practice it means delegating the company, subsidiaries or department's operation, etc., to third parties. This has been conceptually codified by Jensen and Meckling in 1976 under the "agency theory" (Jensen and Meckling, 1976). The corollary is punishment or reward. When the authority has been delegated to a manager, if he or she performs or even overachieves, he or she must be rewarded accordingly; and if he or she fails, he or she must be punished/demoted or fired. The concept is apparently universal. Is it in reality?

Western societies will culturally consider the individual's perform-ance. This is particularly true for societies with a high PDI and a high individualistic factor as defined in the Hofstede scale. In many soci-eties, such as Africa, Asia, Middle East, there is a more "collectivist" mode. This means that reward systems, which are supposed to be the ultimate outcome of controls systems are bound to high risks of fail-ure when they are geared towards individual performance. Rewarding or punishing an individual for his or her performance tends to single out this individual; this is culturally opposite to a paradigm where the individual is a part of a group, and where the whole group should be punished or rewarded. In other words within many world societies, which actually make up the vast majority of the world, the individual reward/punishment system does not operate, and worse still, it tends to create confusion and be counterproductive in the end, yet many MNCs still use it since they copy/paste their own "homeland" cultural traits (individualism).

The same applies to societies which are "feminine" as Hofstede calls them (one can substitute the concept of "farmer" for feminine and hunter for "masculine", because this creates less confusion in practice about the very nature of the concept itself). Thus, "farmer" culturally driven peo-ple, such as in Denmark and the Netherlands, are bound to favour the collective consensus transparent-based decisions as opposed to high PDI autocratic and plutocratic style. This "egalitarian" way is deep-rooted in the culture of these societies. The author also experienced the same in the Pacific Rim originating cultures, where the group was an essential element associated to the tradition.

The World Values Survey" is an organisation that periodically carries out a mapping of "values" on earth. They came out with the Inglehart–Welzel Cultural Map of the World, named after its author Ronald Inglehart. Briefly, it scans the cultures according to two basic dimensions:

(1) Survival (basic needs as per the Maslow pyramid)/self-expression (highest in the Maslow pyramid).
(2) Traditional values (religious)/secular rational values.

It was found that Africa and Asia would be mostly survival- and tradition-driven, whereas Latin America would be tradition-driven but with moderate self-expression. And ex-communist countries (ex-USSR) would be on a survival values mode coupled with a relatively high level of secular orientation. Catholic Europe would be balanced between tradition and secular and is relatively high on the self-expression value; Protestant Europe would be high on secular and self-expression and English-speaking countries would be high on self-expression and balanced between secular and tradition. Inglehart advocated that over time there is a drift by which all societies will become secular and self-expressed.

However, only looking at the recent developments in the Middle East and Asia Minor this is highly debatable.

In summary it is not sufficient for a control mechanism to be based only on a single cultural model, because it may defeat the purpose of increasing efficiency.

Most of the time control systems originate from a culture, and it is mostly the Anglo-Saxon culture because the models and theories are devised first in American business schools and/or American MNCs and later "rolled out" over to the "rest of the world". Note the expression "rest of the world" was, actually the official wording of a former American MNC where the author used to work, used to designate the non-US and non-European countries. Generally, this results in clashes with the local culture at the implementation phase of these models and their supportive "information systems".

4.7 The "people" versus "numbers" model: How does it affect reporting and controlling?

Some cultures are highly "number-oriented". Controllers are very familiar with this: the famous "reporting" is almost exclusively numbers and sometimes with a little comment on the numbers. Even the balanced scorecards are quantitative most of the time. This is the case because numbers are important to the underlying culture.

Everyone is aware of the slogan "what gets measured gets managed".

However, this is not true. Deming a prominent US professor of Statistics, immediately after World War II, introduced the quality to the Japanese and then moved the concept into a formidable marketing element. He is considered the "father" of the quality and he stated that "97% of American managers spend 97% of their time in measuring things that only represent 3% of what influences a company".

Conversely, there is a common saying in marketing that states "a market is people buying from people, not machines from machines".

Mini case: A world-leading Catering service: The reporting is like the gravy: light or heavy: it all depends on the Cook, not the Cooker

This catering service company employed over 308 000 people in all the major countries (40% in Europe, 40% in North America and 20% in the "rest of the world").

Through a statistical forecast analysis received from all parts of the group, the controller identified patterns in "forecasting behaviours". Cultural attitudes is one of the major dimensions which are useful for an accurate interpretation of all forward-looking information produced within a worldwide company:

– Cultures where power is associated with the function and which are not bothered by uncertainty provide forecasts which are factual and could be qualified as "spontaneously transparent"; any significant new event will be directly reflected in the forecast, whatever the magnitude of the impact; the need to take corrective actions to face the consequences of this event and to evaluate their potential impact are rarely taken into consideration when preparing the forecast. Nordic and Anglo-Saxon countries provide this type of "straightforward" and "uncommitted" forecast.

–   Cultures where power is associated to the individual and which tend to avoid uncertainty provide forecasts which show smooth trends in the update of forecasts and could as such be qualified as "subjectively transparent"; the impact of a new event will be reflected partially in the forecast in order to also include the impact of the actions which will be taken for reducing the new source of uncertainty created by this unexpected event; the forecast must show that the pre-announced performance level will be adhered to. Latin countries provide this type of "personalised" and "committed" forecast.

The foregoing business case illustrates that the outputs in terms of forecasts and budgets are far from being uniform in a large global corporation, although the tools, systems and rules are uniform. In fact they differ largely: "soft factors", i.e., culture, take precedence over the "hard factors", i.e., systems. Taking the catering service's forecast, in a Latin culture, the same hit (negative deviation) versus budget is not reported immediately to its full extent, but instead the "gap" is sectioned throughout the remaining periods, and thus the negative impact is "cushioned". Why?

Because it is unacceptable in the Latin culture (power distance dimension) for a manager not to know what to do, therefore, bringing raw bad news to the corporate with no contingency plan is seen as a form of incompetence. Thus, the bad news will be diluted, whilst a recovery plan is developed in parallel. Also, in Latin culture, uncertainty avoidance is high. Showing a crude gap in the forecast is equivalent to recognising that the future is unpredictable and non-controllable. This is culturally unacceptable. On the contrary, the Anglo-Saxon subsidiaries, would report immediately to full extent for the same negative deviation. Why? Same cultural dimensions at work, power distance and uncertainty avoidance, but working in exactly the opposite direction are the answers.

In Anglo-Saxon countries, the power distance is short: the boss is not the boss sui generis, but has a function to discharge and thus makes decisions. Therefore detailed information is needed. It is as simple as that.

Additionally, the uncertainty avoidance factor is relatively low in the United States and United Kingdom: these cultures accept that the future is largely unpredictable, so a deviation versus a plan is not a mistake or a failure (it can be caused by many external uncontrollable factors). The important point is the reaction and the way to recover; thus the full impact is shown upfront, so that the team can work together to fix it.

This example shows that reporting management does not require only pure technical skills on a worldwide basis. It also requires an understanding of differences in cultural attitudes which is essential for correctly interpreting not only the numbers but also the risks and opportunities associated with any forward-looking information.

However, power distance and uncertainty avoidance are not the only cultural dimensions to be understood and monitored by controllers.

4.7.1　The corporate culture

Much has been said so far about the societies'/countries' cultures and to stress how different they can be is what Hofstede qualifies as "collective mind programming".

However, it is equally important to stress the variety that exists in corporate cultures.

Corporations or more widely speaking organisations have different cultures. However, they not only have different cultures but their cultures also evolve according to time and phases.

Professor Edgar Schein at MIT Sloan School of Management, and Professor Mintzberg, Professor of Management at McGill University of Canada are the two masterminds on corporate culture and organisational culture, respectively.

Schein (2005) looked at the different dimensions (Schein calls them "levels") of a corporation culture like Hofstede did for the countries cultures. He categorised three levels. The first and most cursory level is related to visible attributes such as facilities, furnishings, visible awards, dress code, etc.

The second level deals with the professed culture, exemplified by mission statement, slogans, creeds and values. This is a deeper element.

In the third level the deepest, cultural elements are seen, not displayed. The rules although, very strong, are implicit. They are taboo. The organisational cultural norms are deep-rooted and the imposition to conform may be extremely high, although tacit.

This is the reason that in some organisations there may exist some apparent paradox between what is expressed (level 1) and professed (level 2) externally and what is really going on beneath the surface (level 3).

Mini case: When an engineering company is run by accountants

A world-class French engineering company operating in the oil business has been acquiring other engineering companies over the past years, mainly North American.

This company is very prosperous. Invariably the management of the acquired engineering companies state that they are now part of a group, which is no longer run by engineers but by accountants.

It is a fact that this French engineering company has a very strong "control" structure and it is making its profit by its cost accounting systems and its capacity to re-bill its clients to the penny for minute work in excess of the initial basic contractual bidding and not really its technology capability. It is well known in the profession that their cost tracking system is aligned with a strong dissuasive legal capacity as well; as a result, EBIT and cash flows are therefore outstanding, but their engineering quality is only average. Their culture can be seen by "accountants" on top.

When it comes to organisations, Mintzberg is the acknowledged guru worldwide . Mintzberg professes that all organisations go through phases and models over time. He categorised seven major organisational models:

(1) The entrepreneurial start-up
(2) The machine bureaucracy
(3) The professional bureaucracy
(4) The diversified organisation
(5) The innovative organisation
(6) The missionary
(7) The political organisation.

Getting into more detail, a culture can be associated here, but to each model, which most of the time can be seen as a timed evolution of the same organisation beginning as a start-up and finishing like a political organisation.

It is fairly obvious that the culture of a telecoms start-up is different from the one that prevails at the general secretariat of the United Nations (UN) in New York.

Mintzberg (2005) also considers six basic "parts" of an organisation:

(1) The strategic apex (top management)
(2) The middle line (middle management)
(3) The operating core (operations, processes)
(4) Technostructure (analysts)
(5) Support staff
(6) Ideology (halo of beliefs, traditions, norms, values).

There is a specific culture in all of these parts. The board culture is different from the shop floor culture in many ways. The support function cultures (lawyers, accountants) will be different from operations staff (industrial engineers, supply chain managers, etc.).

Overall, the corporate and organisational cultures are very strong. Like the national/regional cultures they are a collective mind programming. Like the national/regional cultures they are visible for some of their attributes and not so visible for the core elements.

In other words, the controlling function to be effective must also be compliant with organisational and corporate cultures.

Summary

The common belief that all businesses be monitored and controlled in the same way is scientifically wrong. The controlling and monitoring modes with all their attributes are profoundly, intrinsically culturally rooted, i.e., national cultures and corporate and organisational cultures.

Although, culture is something primarily experiential, Hofstede, in the late 1960s, provided a scientific and simple way to categorise the five dimensions and measure cultural traits and differences in a seminal (a Copernican revolution) book *Cultures Consequences* which since then remains unrivalled. Like Hofstede, other authors such as Schein and Mintzberg categorised corporate and organisational cultures which are also very strong and drive the business, thus shaping its control and monitoring mode for greater effectiveness.

References

Hall, E. (1959), The Silent Language.
Hofstede, G. (2001), *Cultures Consequences, Second edition.*
Jensen, M. and Meckling, W. (1976), Theory of the firm, *Journal of Economics* 3, 305–360, .
Lewis, R. (2005), *When Cultures Collide.*
Mintzberg, H. (2005), *Strategy Bites Back.*
Montesquieu, F. (1749), *Théorie des climats, Ésprit des Lois.*
Peters, T. and Waterman, R. (1982), *In Search of Excellence.*
Schein, E. (2005), *Organizational Culture and Leadership.*

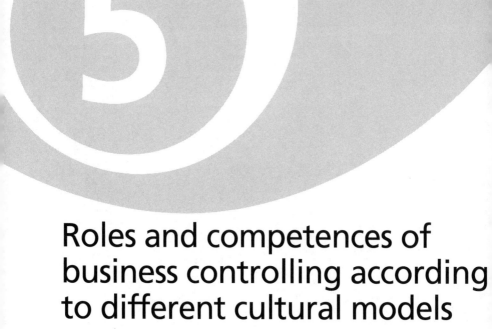

5

Roles and competences of
business controlling according
to different cultural models

This chapter focuses on a typology of different business-controlling modes according to national or regional cultural factors.

It is worth stressing from the beginning that a typology is meant to categorise elements generally and not individually. Thus when discussing the British model, it will not mean that all the British controlling systems or controllers have these characteristics or attributes. It will mean that some key traits do emerge in general and are deep-rooted in the British culture. In Chapter 4, we have been through many cultural dimensions and have seen how they affect and reflect on the way business is carried out, monitored and controlled. Culture, whether corporate or national does impact business and a particular culture is at the core of the way business is conducted.

Six main cultural areas are discussed in this chapter:

(1) Latin
(2) Germanic
(3) British
(4) North American
(5) Scandinavian
(6) Japanese/Asian.

5.1 Latin

The Latin cultural area encompasses nations which were under the Roman rule. The Romans have ruled the world for almost a millennium, from 510 BC to AD 476, in two phases – beginning with the Roman Republic (510 BC to 44 BC date of Julius becoming "Caesar") and afterwards the Empire until its fall in AD 476D due to barbarian invasions from the East. During the thousand years under the Roman rule, the territory was immense stretching from what is now the United Kingdom to the whole of western and southern Europe, Greece, the Balkans, Turkey, eastern Europe, Palestine, Egypt and the Middle East. The entire antique world was Romanised. Interestingly enough the Romans started to be politically organised as a Republic and then moved into dictatorship. An autocratic system headed by an all-powerful Caesar. To understand the lasting impact of Roman rule and the model for its society just consider the word Caesar. Caesar was the title given for absolute power. It gave the word "Kaiser" in German which is still used today, and the Russian word "Tsar" – both meaning "emperor".

Roman rule, varied a great deal over the thousand years, but one can easily imagine its impact over the world. It really shaped the world for a lasting period and its effects are still present in society today. To obtain a reference element one can easily see the influence of the "American way of life" in every aspect of the lives in today's world, although the power and subsequent influence of the United States has only been in place for less than a century (With their entry into World War I, it could be assumed that their influence surpassed British rule over the world). This means 10 times less than the Roman rule, yet the world feels its impact; thus one can imagine the lasting impact of a millennium of Roman influence.

The Roman rule was characterised by, inter alia, two main traits.

The first is what Hofstede would call a high Power Distance Index (PDI) to the extent that, by law, it was the "pater familias" whereby the father in a family had the right over the life or death of his children. This would be rather weird today, but for as long as a millennium it was the law in those days. In practical terms, the father was at the pyramid's summit and the fundamental building brick of the society, that is, the family. There is clearly no place for a "matrix" organisation here. So much for the micro level. At the macro level, the Caesars enjoyed a god-like status, nothing less, thus the top figure of the social organisation was not even an ordinary man any more. His power was absolute with the same magnitude of that of a god. This cultural imprint is still vivid today. In Italy, the word for father and boss is almost the same: padre = father, padrone = boss. This sums it all.

The other main cultural trait that the Latin civilisation brought into the world was the rule of law, and most specifically the Roman law.

Roman law still shapes most of the legal context of continental life in Europe today.

This is the civil law where the law is pre-coded and the judge applies the pre-determined coded punishment, leaving little room for interpretation. Here universalism is the rule.

However, the law in Britain, United States, Canada and most of the ex-British empire is different, being based on common law, meaning that it is essentially precedent based on the sum of all the former individual judges' individual interpretations and decisions which make up the corpus of law on which judgements are based. Here customisation is the rule.

These two main traits have a direct influence on how controlling is performed in Latin countries today, along with two structural dimensions:

(1) The management – fiscal patrimonial accounting dimension (vertical axis)

(2) The norms laws – practice (GAAPs) dimension (horizontal axis).

The Latin controlling style is characterised by a high impact of the law influencing its structure and contents.

Accounting "principles" are not principles anymore per se, they are rules which are part of a law (the accounting law) and thus economic transactions are pre-codified, by law, as are their respective accounting entries and recording mechanisms. There is no room for deviation. Moreover, accounting entries by law must follow a universal coding structure. For example, in France the sales accounting entries must be recorded under an account starting with the figure 7, and each sub-category of sales – product, service, etc. – is sub-coded, as stated by law. The same is with costs; they too have to be encoded as 6, similarly balance sheet accounts, payables are categorised by a 4, and depending on each sub- and sub-category of payables the law provides the minute coding. With only slight differences, the same applies for accounting in Italy and Spain. We can easily recognise the Latin rule here and the spirit of Latin civil law: not only everything is "universally" pre-codified, but the law is in itself also ruling each and every individual accounting transaction coding, and of course no "customisation" or no "industry-specific" is allowed; thus one size fits all. The following section discusses a connection between today's French Plan Comptable and the German accounting tradition in contrast with the Anglo-Saxon spirit (which will be dealt with in more detail later).

As far as the structure is concerned the content is also heavily Latinised. The accounts and thus reporting structures are organised to serve both:

a patrimonial perspective;

a state perspective and most specifically a tax and statistical perspective.

The patrimonial perspective is the dividing line that cuts across the P&L and balance sheet. The fact that a person owns or rents is important: if in France, e.g., a company hires administrative support personnel and employs them directly on their payroll, it is categorised under personnel costs (Frais de personnel) without giving any information as to what purpose or function this personnel hiring is used for. If however the very same personnel are hired using a personnel services company, the accounting entry is categorised under external costs (charges extérieures). This patrimonial perspective helps keep the state and tax and statistical perspective together: one of the main purpose of separating what a person or company has from what it owes is to make very clear what the company must pay to the state; this being apparent in the accounts and records at all times. It is of utmost importance in Latin countries, and especially in France, where 35–40% of the working population is state-employed either directly or through state-controlled agencies and/or state-owned companies. This requires heavy taxes to pay the salary bill of civil servants nationwide (France has one of the highest tax burdens in the whole of Europe and OECD alike). When compared, civil servants represent only 12% in Switzerland, 8% in the United Kingdom and 3% in the United States. Value added is the central element in today's Latin official account organisation. This is why it is important to segregate what is inner (in the foregoing example directly employed personnel) from what is outer (e.g. personnel hired through a service company). To focus on the importance for the state to get a direct and firm grip on the value added, it is important to remember that in continental Europe (being the Latin and Germanic culture nations together) value-added tax (VAT) represents between 65% and 80% of the national revenue, depending on each nation's VAT rate, with France being amongst the highest and Ireland amongst the lowest. Now, it can be understood as to why the continental states insist on enforcing an accounting and reporting structure by law that puts value added at the centre of a company's set of controls; regardless if the value-added concept makes management and control sense or not. And in the immense majority of businesses, value added as a controlling and managerial concept is of no help at all to management and controllers. In Latin and Germanic countries, controlling is therefore not culturally oriented towards management, and in practice there are cultural and systematic difficulties to switch from a "legal" accounting culture to a management accounting culture.

5.1.1 Classical profiles and backgrounds

The classical positioning of controls in Latin countries is heavily on bookkeeping/accounting (general accounting) and is law-/norm-oriented. In general terms it means that little importance is culturally given to management and cost accounting. Therefore, cost and management accounts are derived from the general accounting as a sub-classification called 9, and account (in France) as a sub-product, second-tier element. The primary element being the general/financial/legal accounting. Most of the time the control function is pulled back to basic accounting; furthermore, often bookkeeping discussions and accounting systems are not integrated, leaving a disconnection between general accounting and management accounting (called "analytical" accounting). The role of "Contrôleur de gestion" in French (as in Spain and Italy) is at the crossroads of the role of an accountant being the business analyst and the internal auditor at the same time. The word "Contrôleur de gestion" is very often wrongly and literally translated as "management controller". In practice, the Contrôleur de gestion spends a large part of the time translating "analytical accounting" into proper management accounts (the French even have a name for this translation – "retraitement" which means deep re-processing more than a mere surface restatement) – which leaves little time for analysis and synthesis per se.

In France, the background of these incumbents "Contrôleur de gestion" are typically graduates from the Grandes Ecoles de Gestion (business schools).

5.2 Germanic

Here also history plays a great role in forming cultural traits which in turn profoundly influence business patterns, controls and monitoring. The Germanic cultural area is the result of many centuries of influences, and to go into further detail is beyond the scope of this book. For the purpose of clarity, however, it is important to remember that until the 5th century AD, what is today Germany was partially ruled by the Romans. Like in the rest of the ancient world, their influence was immense and the Latin lex was in force. Following the massive changes in Europe as a consequence of the "Huns" coming from central Asia to invade Europe around AD 400, Germanic-based people such as the Angles and the Saxons fled westward to invade what is today Britain. In AD 800, Carolus Magnus revived the Roman Empire by starting the "Holy Roman Empire of the German nations" or "Holy Roman Empire" which was later put in motion by his descendant, Otto I the Great. This Germanic version of the Roman Empire lasted just less than a millennium ending only recently in the 16th century during the reign of Charles V, having ruled over the whole of Europe with exception of what is now more or less France and the United Kingdom.

In brief, the Germanic countries of today and a vast portion of what is now called eastern Europe was under a mixed influence of Roman/Latin and intrinsic Germanic cultures. No wonder some of the cultural references are so close to the Latin environment, especially when it comes to law and accounting/reporting, thus controlling and monitoring.

The structure of the accounts in German countries today is also precoded by norms and the contents are also heavily taxed and state statistics are oriented like in the Latin world. Incidentally, the word statistics comes from the German "Staatliche information" which means information for the Staat, i.e., the state. This partly explains everything. It is also important to note that in German the word "controlling/monitoring, guiding, driving" is exactly the same word as for the word "tax" – "Steuer". Again it means what it says; the tax dimension is guiding the reporting format, thus the controlling attitude and this is evidence of the deep interconnect (co-substantial) of controlling and state/tax's influence in reporting, and thus the controlling modes. The controlling nature is almost as laws- and norms-oriented as it is in its Latin counterpart, with an extraordinary attention to the minute details, although less patrimonial-oriented, thus its position on the graphic.

The role of controlling is encapsulated in its current German name, "Kostenrechnung", which literally means the "addition of costs". This is the case in traditional German, Swiss German and Austrian firms. In larger international firms, or subsidiaries of MNCs the Anglo-Saxon culture takes over. However, as the industrialisation era started earlier in Germany (and in the United Kingdom) compared to Latin Europe (almost a century later), the industrial accounting as well as its interfaces with the general/financial accounting is more developed, although it retains more of a "bookkeeping" attitude than that of an accounting "spirit". Interestingly enough the Germanic- and the Latin tradition found a formal "expression" in the midst of the 20th century; the accounting structure – chart of accounts – and contents used in Germany (and still mostly in use today) were devised by the Nazis in the 1930s: the German chart of accounts, called the "Goering Chart of accounts". The purpose was to organise a uniform accounting standard so that the whole of the German economy could be planned and controlled efficiently. In 1942, it was introduced in France by the Vichy government, following France's occupation. It has remained in existence parallelly in both countries with little change, thus leaving great similarities in both structures and inspirations/purposes: controlled economy, state control pre-eminence over business and management.

5.2.1 Background

German controllers come mostly from universities with a diplom-kaufmann/frau background as well as via the apprenticeship route in Germany which is excellent.

5.3 British

The British controlling world is quite different from the Latin or the German one. Here again the cultural and historical backgrounds are essential drivers.

The British accounting reference frame is similar to the legal frame, case-based and thus customised. It roots back to Britain's history where there is nothing such as a universal legally codified accounting structure, where the accounts would be specified by an act of parliament.

Instead the practice has, over time, generated generally accepted principles by the profession and adapted to an industry sector. Like the law, it is customised. The purpose of British accounting and controlling is also mostly management- and shareholder interest orientated, and not primarily for the state. In Latin and Germanic accounting, tax accounting is not only strict with financial accounting, but is also at the core of the whole accounting structure and coding, management accounting being only a by-product. However, the key to British accounting is information to management.

This is a radical change in scope: in the United Kingdom, management uses accounting information to make decisions; the tax accounting is mostly kept on a separate ledger.

The structure and contents of the chart of accounts is flexible as long as it shows a fair and true view of the business, however, the P&L and the balance sheet are organised by key business processes most of the time, i.e., straight and right to the point thus:

Cost of goods sold, and not a tortuous combination, such as in the Latin charter of accountants, made of purchases to third parties – to make apparent the sacrosanct value-added concept which is only relevant to state statisticians and taxmen – and inventory variations valued at different levels to adjust back to some sort of "cost of goods sold" that turns into a long winded detour.

- R&D costs which represent the entrepreneurial effort
- Sales and marketing costs which represent a clear-cut key business process
- Administrative costs which represent the weight of the support functions, etc.

This has also to do with the fact that Britain was the first country to move away from an agrarian society to an industrial society by the end of the 18th century and therefore had to develop a comprehensive industrial and entrepreneurial accounting to help management be in control and thus allow business to develop. It has since then remained the primary focus.

5.3.1 Background

Despite the various ways of controlling, there is a pattern. In 1919, the Institute of Costs and Works Accountants, now the CIMA – Chartered

Institute of Management Accountants – was created to provide professional training to those who wanted to become management accountants, and later controllers. At the beginning this body was unique to the United Kingdom, but is now highly regarded throughout the world as one of the best qualified training institute.

Not only is the classical charter/certified accountant qualifications highly regarded but also the training that provides excellent background for controlling in the United Kingdom as well as worldwide. Despite this, certified and chartered accountants are found mostly in auditing firms or functions where they excel worldwide.

5.4 North American

Firstly, it is important to note that the United States ranks first for the individualistic characteristics according to the Hofstede scale, and in the first quartile for masculinity (in the sense of hunter versus farmer). This of course shapes the attitude towards controlling, which roots back to American collective history. For example, the individual performance tracking and rewarding is a characteristic of the classical American business model, perfectly coherent with the social values of the United States. This is held true at all levels of the organisation, from the commission paid to the sales representative, to the stock options given to high ranking officers and executives.

This monitoring system is not true and valid everywhere.

Mini case: When a "tip" does not buy the "top"

When I started working in France, 30 years ago, for a large American multinational, I was a young business analyst in charge of budgeting. In this role I had discussions with the sales director, a very professional Frenchman in his field and respected by his clients, suppliers and competitors alike. One day, surprised at seeing that the line "bonus" was left blank, I enquired as to why this was the case. The French sales director came with an immediate and straightforward answer.

He told me that this was no mistake, and that it was left voluntarily blank because all the sales team members were dedicated to what they did. The sales director explained "They do their very best day in, day out and they are paid for that. They are proud of what they do and the company they are working for and are loyal to it. Paying them a 'tip' on top of their salary would mean that I consider them, as non-performing by themselves in normal time, and that I have to pay extra for them to start real work". This meant that it would not only be taken as a straight insult to their sense of loyalty and their sense of dedication, by introducing individual rewards, but would also break the team into pieces forever. It would turn out to be ultimately unproductive. When this discussion was over, I went back to my office and traced back the sales statistics for this department. As a team they had enjoyed an unbroken record of sales revenues over the past 10 years. Moreover their client fidelity ratio was the best across the whole corporation in Europe. Finally, this business way of monitoring was perfectly coherent with the prevailing local culture.

Given the weight of the American economy and stock exchange in the world, the accounting methods, the US GAAPs are de facto the world rule. This has complicated practical consequences, in particular, within the foreign subsidiaries of US groups, because those subsidiaries have to regularly feed the consolidation systems to their US parents by reporting as per US GAAPs in USD, mostly on a monthly basis but they were also bound by law to keep their local statutory books in local currencies and as per local legal accounting regulations (often called the local GAAPs). This begs the question as to whether these foreign subsidiaries of the US MNCs are better off keeping their basic books and recording their day-to-day transactions directly in US GAAPs as if they were neither in Paris nor in Shanghai but somewhere in the middle of North Dakota, and "translate" from US GAAPs back into their local requirement, as a by-product, to comply with local regulations and reporting, or should they record their day-to-day transactions and keep their current books in local "GAAPs" and, keeping it aside, compile the US GAAP's report?

After 30 years of experience in a variety of groups, I have found no 'pre-mix" answer to this point. Some guidelines could however be drawn and followed:

Complying with local accounting, tax laws and reporting obligations is not negotiable.

Volume is an important determinant as an input to the decision making on which solution to choose.

Maintaining local books on by-side spreadsheets and macros, whilst the core data is carried out the US GAAP's way, or vice versa is rarely a good and never a stable solution. But it can help at the beginning and during transition phases. The best solution is to make entries in both set of books (local and US GAAPs) simultaneously using one single entry modules/facilities.

Mini case: The day the whole accounting vanished

Has any CFO ever had the nightmare that all the basic accounting vanishes with no accounting record left?

This has happened in a small subsidiary of a giant US corporation in Spain. The local controller used to keep all accounting records and transaction directly in US GAAPs. He was an American national, and an American CPA (Certified Public Accountant); thus for him this was natural to do. As a matter of detail his reporting to the United States was flawless and always on time. Eleven months after he took the job, he died in a car accident. A replacement controller of another division of the same US group was immediately sent from Madrid to Barcelona for continuity. It was the period for submitting local statutory books and tax books to the local Spanish authorities, and to the replacement controller's great surprise there were just no local books, not even the slightest local bookkeeping. It was stressful, to say the least. What had happened? Right from the beginning the US CPA controller had decided that since he had to report on a monthly basisto the United States in minute detail, it would be better to keep all records under US GAAPs, and once a year build a "little" spreadsheet and macro-engineered interface module to translate the US accounting into Spanish statutory and tax books when necessary. He had no real idea of how complex this would actually be since he had never worked in Spain before. He died before this could ever happen. As a result the subsidiary had no valid accounting in Spain and was infringing the law, to an extent where this engaged the personal liability of its CEO. There was no other alternative but to reconstruct the whole legal and local tax books from scratch: a costly and cumbersome task, not to speak of the trouble with the local authorities.

The second notable exception has to deal with the positioning of the controlling and monitoring function.

In the United Stated, the controller's role is close to that of a financial director, excep that the cash management–related functions are assigned to a treasurer most of the time, who does not report to the controller (the separation of duties help maintain sound internal control). In brief the US controller is in charge of "producing the numbers", and in particular the cost and managements accounts, which, given the prevailing high level of qualification, is perfectly well done most of the time.

Apart from the classical controller's role of reporting to the business management unit, there exists the role of "business analyst". This role is at the interface between the controller's role and the line management role. It consists of analysing the internal accounting data, with a focus on cost and management accounts, in combination with external data (sales, competition, prices, exchange rate, market share, etc.) to produce sound and profound analyses, scenario, forecasts, trends, plans, investments cases, etc.

5.4.1 Background

Generally, controllers are CPA-qualified with significant industry experience. This is, broadly, the US equivalent of the British chartered or certified accountants. Their career evolves frequently towards the CFO role. Although, the business analysts frequently come from business school backgrounds (MBA, Masters in Management) coupled with an engineering- or a law background, their career prospects are in business and line management, and eventually lead towards the CEO or a similar role. Pro memoria, the role and influence of controlling and the business analysis function is paramount in US MNCs.

5.5 Scandinavian

Denmark, Norway and Sweden are the Scandinavian countries, and although Finland is not geographically speaking part of Scandinavia, it can be culturally associated with them. The Baltic countries – Lithuania, Estonia and Latvia – can be connected to the Scandinavian rim in terms of culture. As stated earlier, it is important to remember that the Scandinavian countries rank very low in the "masculinity" index as per Hofstede and also have a very low PDI. In other words, they are nations with a "farmer" attitude and where the "egalitarian" and consensus perspective are key social pillars. In this context, the word "controller" in itself is not even commonly employed in businesses as it conveys a sense of rigid rules, distrust, power, audit, etc. Instead the word "economist" is used, and since we now know that words are not neutral, the functions of an economist are different from that of a controller. The economist has a function where the "business economics", not management accounting, is at the centre in that the corporation is most of the time seen and expressed in a systemic view. Relationships from cause to effect are important and seen in "cold" and "scientific view" – an "engineer's view".

Mini case: Hocus pocus spells ABC in Sweden

Twenty-five years ago, two engineers at Ericsson were employed as "economists" to determine the different costs of each product within the company. They were not satisfied with the current overhead and fixed costs allocations methods currently used. As 80% of costs were "fixed", variations in allocation "keys" would make one business line profitable one day and catastrophic the next day . They then applied their engineer and "system" mind to track the cause and effect in some sort of canonical "factors" that they identified as activities. Activity was the driver of costs to them, even if those costs were reputed by accountants to be fixed, they were actually considered not to be so. They then decided to create their own consulting firm based on this revolutionary "system" thinking, called "profitability tracking". They applied it to a Swedish special steel factory. They invited scholars to look at their new "discovery" and soon scholars from America's Harvard Business School used the steel factory example, with their agreement, to teach it as a business model and popularised it through the famous acronym ABC (Activity Base Costing). ABC (Johnson and Kaplan, 1987) has now spread across the globe and is working like magic and is the hocus pocus word for sorting out and cutting across the complex profitability maze in corporations.

5.6 Japanese/Asian

When entering the Asian and Japanese world we step into a different scenario, totally different from the Western-based business models. In far eastern societies, time is a fundamental pillar. This penetrates every aspect and space. Time is abundant, things can improve or change over centuries, which of course does not mean that things cannot be expedited quickly when it is decided to do so. Time has an elasticity factor that has no equivalent in the West, except may be in Africa. For the Western-based business models, as well as long-term commitment, this is another dimension. For example, three business sectors that Asians and particularly Japan decided to develop post-World War II are consumer electronics, photography and automotive. In these three sectors, they started from nothing: no technology, no resources, no brand, no marketing and no distribution channels. The major giants of those days were RCA, Kodak and General Motors, to name a few. Even using today's Western business school models, the "entry barriers" would have been considered too high to give them the slightest chance of success. The calculation on the return on investment period over an average of 3 years ROCE would have turned out to be catastrophic, even without considering that in those early days all the other red signals, investment were nevertheless committed, and the first decades accumulated losses. However, 60 years later the Asians and the Japanese, in particular, are the world leaders today, by all standards, in every industrial sector.

Why?

Because of at least two fundamental cultural factors:

The concept of time and commitment to long-term goals, regardless of early difficulties or setbacks. Here the culture of long term means long term, not just looking to the next quarter as dictated by the stock exchange.

Collectivism: In general, Asian societies are collective in essence. The group is the building brick, not so much the individual. It is only because groups can be put into motion and kept advancing over a long period of time so that extraordinary results can be achieved.

As this is the way to conduct business in Asia, coupled with the aspects discussed earlier regarding the "networking", be it Guanxhi in China, Keiretsu in Japan or Choebol in Korea, a very different style in controlling is necessary. This is particularly the case of "remote" controlling per se as understood in the West, where the subsidiary that is disconnected from the major company would be completely alien in the East. As was discussed earlier, the culture commands that "all is in all". Analytically slicing and dicing the functions as it is done in the West is a pure mental construct for Asians, which is against their vision of the world. The Asian's vision of the world is fundamentally "holistic", the best example being traditional Asian medicine, be it Chinese or Indian, unlike the West's vision of the world which is analytical, disconnected and of a highly conceptual/abstract nature. Thus, to fit this cultural requirement of the Asian society, the "control" in Asia, if it exists at all, must be culturally embodied in the business processes itself, not outside of it.

Mini case: The Toyota Way

Toyota has pioneered and developed the Toyota Production System (TPS), which is now famous and known as "kan ban" or "lean manufacturing" which is a combination of "just in time" and "kaizen" (continuous improvement). For Toyota there is no such thing as an external "control" to monitor business. It is considered as a pure misconception. Since culturally "all is in all", the control function should not even exist, it would just prove that the process was wrong. Instead the process must be self-controlled at each micro stage. If the process is correct, then the production is correct and the whole system harmonious. An ex-post-control is a cultural nonsense. Kan ban is exactly that: the control information flows physically and intrinsically with the product. The controls are physical and visual. The concept of an "information factory" does not exist as is currently found in Western corporations where data is disconnected from the products, then converted into abstract financial aggregates, and re-converted into the so-called management accounts/information, whilst most of the substance having been lost or diluted in the process, without taking into consideration the substantial time lag occurring between a business event which takes place and its capture on listing print outs. The Toyota system is a whole and was called the TPS for years, and constantly and consistently explained that the whole Toyota group's philosophy was self-contained in this TPS. However, they realised that Americans and Europeans had a limited understanding of the TPS system in the course of their international development; Americans and Europeans mimicked what their analytical eyes and brains could see: the discrete "gizmos" like the Andon cord. They invested time and effort to reproduce the widgets and gadgets like the pokey yoke, they replicated the visible part of the TPS iceberg, the only ones that they could see, and they failed. They failed because they all fail to capture the cultural side of TPS, the "spiritual values" which are culturally deep-rooted. Transplanting the tree – the gizmos – without transplanting the earth and soil – the culture – was the mistake. The Toyota way based on the "all is in all" cultural drivers, is not just an alternate hypothetical "exotic" way. It is the holistic philosophy that propelled Toyota to the top position in the world automotive business, as well as the number one on US soil. Toyota stock value surpasses that of GM, Ford and Chrysler together, whilst still making profit whereas, Ford and GM are making record losses. GM and Ford have based their culture on dissection of tasks and "hard" controlling, the very classical Western way. GM and Ford were so iconic to the Western management, serving as "universal" role models that the reputed business school MIT named "the Sloane School of Management" after the first CEO of General Motors.

Summary

Putting typologies together is never correct by definition. Any typology reduces the peculiarities of an infinite variety to a common denominator, and that is as wrong as taking the mean average as a single figure that sums up the whole spread of the reality in a single digit. The result is the risk to be so reductive as to produce "clichés" and stereotypes. However, typologies do help to see through and make relative the very often "one sizes fits all" approach. This"one size fits all approach" is called "ethnocentrism", which means that we tend to see the world in relation to our own culture and then go on to categorise what we believe is correct or good and what is incorrect or bad. This is particularly true with controlling and monitoring businesses. In fact there are as many "correct" controlling philosophies (thus systems) as there are cultures. This chapter has shown a few typologies of controlling and monitoring businesses, and we have seen that they all differ both in substance (the "what" is controlled) and in style (the "how" is controlled). We have also seen that those systems were congruent with the social values and cultures from which they originate. We have also recognised that the corporate culture is a key determinant in the way business is conducted and managed. The connection between corporate- and national cultures has also been identified as a major area of potential conflicts and clashes in MNCs, whereas if they are adequately managed they represent a formidable lever to profit. The world is becoming increasingly international today, not because there are more nations that pop up everyday, but because the fluxes of goods and capital (and to a much lesser extent of people) between counties and region is increasing in an unprecedented way. In the majority of cases, however, the business controlling and monitoring models taught and practised are still those that once fitted the Western, mainly North American, culture. This clash between actual diversity and dreamed uniformity is a challenge for the controller at the beginning of the 21st century.

References

Johnson, H.T. and Kaplan, R. (1987), Relevance Lost.

How should business controlling be shaped to best fit with phases of internationalisation dynamics, cultures and critical factors?

6.1 The different patterns

Mini case: Is the world flat? Has history ended?

These sound like weird questions that most of us thought had been solved centuries ago, but obviously not for everyone. North American scholars recently revived old questions came up saying in their thesis that after the Berlin wall had fallen, the world was only left with one ideology, so there was no history anymore, all was achieved. This is in direct contrast to what Marx (Marx, 1867) said, being inspired from Hegel (Hegel, 1817); it was not communism but capitalism that was the universal sense of history, the sole remaining "philosophical" value since the ultimate "winner takes all": quod erat demonstrandum. As "convergence" has become the new ideology through easier communications (Internet) and massive off shoring, making the earth without boundaries, all the more so that the ex-communist countries such as Russia, China and Eastern Europe have all embraced a common "faith" in capitalism (called liberalism). The world is then considered finitely "flat". From a pure scientific point of view, history has not ended and will never end, except at the eschatological end of time – if that ever happens. Ironically other physically dividing walls have been built in other parts of the world since the one in Berlin fell, parting off nations, being just as long and as high as the Berlin one was, e.g., the Mexican–US border, Palestine–Israel. Is history repeating itself? Moreover the world is a sphere, a globe, not flat. American taxpayers have poured trillions of dollars to prove this by funding for the sending of satellites into orbit for more than half a century.

Mini case: Is the "Globe" global?

This sounds like another stupid question, but is it really?

The concept of globe comes from the sphere itself and makes reference to a sphere seen from a distance by an "outside" observer. The further a person is from the sphere the less the details can be seen, the more the sphere appears "globally" uniform with no granularity – bald. In Latin-based languages the word "global" (globus in Latin, globalité in French, globalidad in Spanish, etc.) means totality: the whole in opposition to the details, the whole over the detail. Therefore in essence, the meaning of globalisation exactly opposite to that of internationalisation. Internationalisation means exactly what it says: internations, it focuses on the exchanges, fluxes, relations between nations, recognising their diversities – distinct, diverse nations (thus cultures). Globalisation simply denies the diversity, be it within nations, cultures, languages, philosophies or flora and fauna. Globalisation is a concept that equates to uniformity. The question should be which original social model should be used as the one to be cloned to achieve a worldwide uniformity? What about the non-conforming/non-complying elements? Should they be "reworked" until they eventually "converge" or are simply "scrapped"? Across history, the world has already experienced many "flatteners", such as Darius, Nero, Attila, Genghis Khan, Torquemada, Cortes, Pisaro, Napoleon, Stalin, Hitler and Pol Pot. They were all proponents of the "convergence" theory.

The world is definitely not flat, but there is a real risk, perhaps more than ever before to "flatten" it by depleting it forever. This will be discussed in the forthcoming chapters.

In the former chapters it has been seen how different patterns and phases of the internationalisation process and the immense weight MNCs can very often outweigh sovereign states. Most of the MNCs are US-originated as one can easily see from any "Fortune 500" type ranking. Fewer are European, and even fewer are Asian, African or Middle Eastern. This means focusing on the two dominant management styles of MNCs: American and European. It is more difficult to establish typologies for the others as there are not so many in existence that count as economic heavyweights. But they are coming fast (India, China, Brazil, etc.).

6.2   The North American MNC's business style and controlling attitude

North American MNCs follow the general phased approach as discussed in Chapter 3. However, they have their own way that is driven by cultural traits typical of their homeland in the United States. Naturally their respective corporate cultures play a great role, but the national cultural drivers take precedence. Those typical cultural traits can be associated with the Hofstede's five dimensions. In practice this results in self-confident/assertive organisations and projects their own cultural model of a high "hunter"/"masculine" score combined with high individualism in the foreign countries they operate. Another characteristic is their organic coherence. These American organisations very often have a uniquely strong combination of a national domestic culture and corporate culture. This coherence exists because national domestic values are aligned with corporate values, and therefore corporate and domestic cultures are mutually reinforced. It must be noted that at this point the US domestic culture is extremely uniform. Culture and values are fairly identical to a person in North Dakota or North Carolina, Chicago or New York. There might be some minor variations, but overall, the domestic cultural traits are uniform. The root cause of this uniformity is to be understood in the history of the formation of the United States. Furthermore, uniformity is scripted on the Great Seal of the United States: E Pluribus Unum. The first letter "E" of this Latin language expression stands for "ex" which means literally out of, from, as the result of. The second word Pluribus means diversity, plurality and the third word Unum means one in neutral form, like a one "thing". The verb – est meaning "is" – is voluntarily omitted to stress on the direct confrontation of diversity even more and its transformation into a one element: pluribus/unum: there is room for nothing in between, not even for a verb: one is either in or out of the mould. This clearly means what it says: from the vast diversity let us reduce to uniformity. To reinforce the image, the "melting pot" was also used, which projects the idea of different elements destroyed in their chemical integrity to form a new single alloy – from natural diversity to artificial (the melting process) uniformity. Here there is no need to elaborate on the way to deal with diversity any further: melting is the answer, the only best way. American MNCs therefore tend to consciously stress on the corporate culture: they pioneered the corporate "messianic" CEO's visions, corporate charters, corporate creeds, strict procedures, systematic personal "evaluations" resulting in gauging the "performance" and the degree of conformity to the mould of every single employee whether in their behaviour or in their "career" aspirations.

Unconsciously through rites and rituals such as the "Friday wear", the casual dress code, as the likes of the famous Arthur Andersen grey suit, the IBM black tie, or from the Silicon valley casual fit to the auditors compulsory Friday wear (same charcoal suit as the other week days but no tie) including the corporate myths and heroes, like the "employee of the month" to the extent of sometimes even having a full-fledged pantheon of them to the famous storytelling and "experience sharing" of the corporate mythology of today. Even the sacrosanct monthly reporting serves much more than just a simple cause of "reporting" figures back to the Parent company. It also repeats the old ritual of "communicating" with the higher entities (like the communion with the gods). The list would be too long to go into further detail, but keep in mind that controlling and behavioural monitoring are high. They are at the core of the controlling and monitoring procedures. As a matter of consequence the degree of consistency in the whole American MNC is high, and allows it to act rapidly and decisively in a consistent and uniform manner all over the world. This is of course a very valuable advantage vis à vis the competition, at least in the short run. Control is highly financial by nature and centralised most of the time. Parent decides and the subsidiaries execute. It derives a real force and a radiating energy from this, especially when it comes to "roll out" worldwide programs or projects. The word "roll out" speaks also for itself. It implies or means to "bulldozer" out the programme. In Latin-speaking countries the word used is "déployer" in French or "desarollar" in Spanish. This very same word is used for a flower, a fruit, or a human being that develops harmoniously over time. In one word the entire difference in the way programmes are controlled from the United States and Latin and Mediterranean perspective can be understood. The language used in American MNCs is uniformly English, American English being a plus, conferring a distinctive status comparable to the one that Roman citizenship conferred to non-Roman citizens as well as to non-Roman born, but individuals Romanised enough. American education plays a similar role. In practice, a bachelor from any third tier US University will be conferred a higher status (even to a non-US native) than a PhD from France's famous Sorbonne University in terms of career advancement.

Mini case: When time was the same around the world: New York Time as the Universal Time all over the world ...

In the 1970s, a now defunct American MNC, which was extremely famous at the time, decided that to "officially" optimise the usage of time for the higher ranking officers from the US HQ visiting Europe, and the "rest of the world"; all of the corporation's clock worldwide would be set to New York time which was where this particular MNC had its headquarters. In practical terms this meant that business meeting in the European subsidiary would physically have to take place in the middle of the night, everyone pretending that it is was lunch time just like in New York! This saved the American executives from re-adjusting to the time zones in the "rest of the world" but it served the cause of reinforcing control – control on the financials and minds.

6.3 The European MNC

Before discussing the typical European way of doing and controlling business, it is important to define what Europe is and what it is not. Europe is not geographically defined, neither is it politically nor culturally defined. Its common denominator is variety and not uniformity.

Geographically Europe is a blurred notion. At best it can be defined as the extreme western extremity of the Asian continent. If forced to be more specific, one could see some natural "boundaries" that delimit the European area. On the east these are the Urals Mountains (east from Moscow) and on the south the Mediterranean Sea with Greece, and part of the Black Sea, at the exclusion of Turkey which is geographically located in Asia (Asia Minor).

Europe does not exist politically per se either. There is no European nation, nor is there any European state despite recent enforced attempts to create the "United States of Europe" which has blatantly failed in some countries where a people's vote was organised under a referendum.

The countries are extremely diverse in size, history, culture, economics and demographics, but have concluded mutually binding treaties, mainly of a commercial and financial nature which organises the European Union (EU), where goods and financial flows circulate freely. In 2007, the EU comprised 27 member states that have for centuries been at war with each other. Europe includes 7 monarchies, 3 ex-Fascist states and 10 ex-Soviet Republics or communist bloc countries. In 2006, 13 member states decided to share the euro as a common currency, and 15 states adopted the Schengen Agreement that allowed Europeans to move freely from one member state to the other. Some member states are members of NATO whereas others are not.

In terms of governance, the EU as a whole takes directives or regulations that are to a greater or lesser degree then "transposed" into local national law by local parliaments. It is estimated that up to 70% of national laws are in fact mere "transpositions" of EU directives, where some countries apply the letter of the law and some, mainly the Latin-cultured states, the spirit of the law. It is an interesting point to note that the initiative of the EU directives is with the European Commission, which is a non-elected body composed of 27 co-opted individuals. Approximately, one per member state, but this is subject to change. The Commission directives are the result of an intensive preparation work by the supporting EU technical groups, the so-called "expert" committees which are often targeted by powerful lobbies of all sorts. Moreover the "rules" for approving or rejecting directives are fluctuating and extremely complicated, leaving much room for coalition and inner political alliances. In summary, the EU is a non-state governed like a would-be state or a would-be supranational democracy, by 27 diverging "real" nations, and the core "law" directives are initiated by a non-elected body of 27 individuals, heavily "targeted" by groups of lobbyists through the so-called "expert committees".

Culturally "Europe" is one of the most fragmented "regions" in the world.

Europe spreads all along the spectrum on every single Hofstede's cultural dimension, e.g.,France ranks the highest in terms of Power Distance Index (PDI), with the high score of 68; whereas Austria ranks one of the lowest in the world at the 53rd position with a score of as low as 11.

Greece is the most adverse nation to uncertainty in the world in terms of Uncertainty Avoidance Index (UAI), with a UAI of 112; whereas Denmark has one of the lowest score in the world with a UAI of just 23.

In terms of individualism, Great Britain scores as high as 3rd in the world and 1st in Europe with a high mark of 89, whereas Greece scores as low as the 30th position with a score of only 35.

In terms of masculinity (hunters), Austria ranks 2nd in the world and 1st in Europe with an index as high as 79, whereas Sweden is the lowest country in the world, the more "farmer style" and an index as low as 5.

Europe is totally fragmented culturally with no coherence whatsoever that would tend to characterise a common "European cultural character". Culturally Europe is immensely varied, at odds with the coherence of the United States, obtained via the "melting pot" process.

6.3.1 Language

Europe is a region with many languages, totalling over a hundred different languages and dialects. Naturally this variety of languages reflects the variety in cultures. The author of this book writes and speaks six languages and is very sensitive to languages in the way they shape thinking. No concept is "universal". It has a home and this home is the language in which it has been initially "taught"; language is itself influenced by the culture.

An example of a European country by excellence is Switzerland, although not part of EU. This country is located geographically in the centre of Europe, and has enjoyed stability, peace, harmony and prosperity for almost a millennium. Four official languages are spoken in Switzerland – Romansch (the last descendant of Latin still actively spoken), Italian, French and German more commonly known in reality as Swiss German. Swiss German is a dialect that is derived from the official German language, which has approximately 60% commonality, with strong divergence in pronunciation. There is actually not a single Swiss German language, but many Swiss German dialects spread over the many cantons whereby there are sometimes even several dialects by canton. There are about 21 dialects. Are they all really different? In fact they are; their degree of mutual commonality is 60%. Every dialect has its legitimacy and is a strong component of the identity. More interesting is a recent analysis carried out by the federal government revealing that far from being less spoken, the Swiss German dialects are spoken more frequently particularly amongst the younger generation. They are proud of their identity and heritage and wish to express it. Likewise in the French-speaking part of Switzerland, the "Romandie" region, the French spoken is not the same as spoken in France. It has multiple variations in grammar, vocabulary and pronunciation. Once again, Swiss French is not uniform, but varies across the country depending on whether one is in Geneva, Lausanne, Sion or Neuchatel. Although Switzerland is a small country with regard to size, it is a great country in the sciences, human rights, economics, arts and humanities aspect. It is a rich country too, not only cash rich, but in talent and variety.

German is the language that is spoken the most in Europe, with almost a hundred millions speakers, followed by English, French and Italian, on par with roughly 60 million speakers each. If therefore the EU should align itself on one common language, it should be German. It is estimated on an average that 1 European out of 10 can express himself or herself in another foreign language (in 50% of cases English is the preferred "second language"), and less than 0.1% of the Europeans can express themselves in 2 European languages other than their mother tongue. This coupled with the fact that only 1% of Europeans live in a European country other than their country of origin, one can immediately see that the language variety is a major European trait. Variety, not uniformity is therefore the rule. For obvious reasons, however, it is believed that English is Europe's most commonly used language. However, in corporations this often leads to disastrous scenarios:

Mini case: The Tower of Babel has its homeland in Europe

An internal communication is to be delivered within a company. The originator is a Latvian national (an EU member state) who "masters" above average English. He elaborates his communication in English (assuming that few, if any, of his colleagues around the table speak Latvian). Only 25% of the contents are lost in his translation which can be considered to be excellent. At the meeting, his female colleague from Germany, who speaks decent English, "captures" 67% of what he said. She then discusses the point with her neighbour sitting on her left, a Frenchman of Moroccan descent, who also speaks fluent Arabic, but "struggles" with English. He manages to only understand 50% of the contents at best. The bottom line is that in just the first circle of this typical "European" meeting only 22.5% of the initial Latvian's contents had passed through the "language" barrier. Language is a key element in managing European MNCs, most of the time language clumsiness is purely and simply denied because recognising it would be "untrendy" (i.e., politically incorrect). Amongst the few top executives whom the author met, who completely acknowledged the variety of languages in Europe as a business subject to tackle, was the top executive of Toyota.

Corruption variation

Corruption levels are extremely varied in Europe, ranging from virtually non-corrupted countries, such as Finland, Norway, Sweden and generally the Nordic Rim countries, to countries where corruption is so high that organised crime is a societal pillar (southern Europe) and a leading economic sector (estimated to be as much as 10% of GDP in Italy). In terms of corporate governance this means that cultural perceptions are necessarily extremely different.

6.3.2 Economics

Europe is again extremely varied and fragmented when it comes to economics.

The "Global Competitiveness Index" in 2003 displayed European countries ranging from the best to the worst in the world. As an example:

(1) USA
(2) Finland
(3) Luxembourg
(4) The Netherlands
(5) Denmark

(15) Germany

(22) France

...

(36) Spain

(37) Slovakia

(38) Slovenia

In terms of the Human Development Index (HDI),Norway ranks 1st, whereas Bulgaria is at the 56th position.

In terms of GDP per capita in PPP (purchasing power parity), the spread is again immense: world ranking for 2003 is as follows:

(1) Luxembourg – 133

(2) USA – 100

(3) Switzerland – 89

(4) Norway – 86

(5) Iceland – 84

(6) Belgium – 80

(15) Germany – 73

(19) France – 72

(21) UK – 69

(61) Latvia – 21

(63) Lithuania – 20

(65) Romania – 19

Europe of 27 states GDP per capita in PPP (rounded up to 100%) is on average 60, whereas the United States stands at 100; thus almost half by comparison, although the European population is 500 million whereas that of United States is only 300 million.

One immediately sees that "Europe" has no "coherent" genes, and even less uniform ones. It is its variety not its homogeneity that makes Europe European.

Now that Europe has been briefly characterised, let us focus on the "European" MNC.

Breiefly, there are four main types of European MNCs:

(1) The MNC that stems from a strong long-established corporation, such as Philips from the Netherlands, or British Petroleum from

the United Kingdom, or BASF from Germany, (an off spring of IG Farben conglomerate one of the most powerful corporation during the Nazi period), FIAT of Italy or Scania of Sweden. They are based on a tradition of entrepreneurs and financiers that started as family businesses and expanded internationally, becoming eventually world heavyweight MNCs.

BP started in 1901 under William Knox d'Arcy; the Agnelli family founded FIAT in 1899; Gerard Philips, a cousin of Karl Marx, founded Philips in 1891; the Wallenberg family founded Scania in 1865 and BASF was also founded in 1865.

In many ways they resemble the classical North American corporations in that they are homogeneous and have a homeland-centred management: home tropism. They have homogeneity and a strong corporate culture with coherent decision-making.

(2) The national "champions" coming typically from once or still nationalised companies, which under the new EU directive "creed" have to "open up" for "open competition". It is interesting to note that all recent analyses have tended to prove that the opening up of sectors like communications or transportation to competition that were formerly state owned, or where service selling prices were state regulated, have resulted in favouring the emergence of private monopolies or oligopolies, driving up the services selling price on the market rather up than down as initially "predicted" by the EU Commission. These companies have both a very strong national culture and a domestic mentality. France with almost one third of its GDP based on totally or partially stated-controlled companies is an excellent example of this. Moreover these companies have a tradition of mixing up politics and governance as they were originating from key economic- or defence-related sectors.

Mini case: EDF: The French Electricity company and Alstom

EDF stands for Electricté de France. It was nationalised after World War II and although it ranked 63rd in the world (Fortune 500), it is largely a domestic operator. It has to internationalise its operations under the EU directive opening up to the free competitive market. It achieves this mainly through acquisitions but remains domestically centred at its core to the extent that the French state interferes to avoid any takeover of EDF by a non-French operator, thus pushing for the Franco French "champion solution".

The French giant Alstom recently underwent the same treatment despite international criticism of the French government's blatant intervention to save the bankrupted firm from disappearing from the French economy and international arena during the sensitive run up to the recent 2007 presidential elections. In an effort to halt social unrest in an already high unemployment situation, the French government invested heavily to realign this ex-nationalised industry which has, amongst other things, the virtual monopoly on manufacturing trains for the French railways.

(3)   The bicultural multinational giants of long-standing joint history:

These industries are scarcer today but prove to be very robust and economically efficient. These are, inter alia, the Anglo Dutch Royal Dutch Shell that has developed an international presence by virtue of a dual "citizenship" being well thought out and where cultural variety is not only mastered but also used as a leverage having been nurtured for over a century; similar is the case with Unilever.

(4)   The artificially "composed" medium-size European MNCs made up of multiple components resulting from the strata of former acquisitions and divestures and re-agglomerated "debris" and leftovers of otherwise former coherent groups (divested plants, spun off divisions, rationalised enterprises, etc.). They are the most numerous. Typically, they are rather recent corporations which have gone through different phases of acquisitions fuelled by funds (or fund management) and which under the EU ideology are examples of total capitalism (called liberalism). These "coagulation" of company "cells" have taken up different forms. Most started by divestment of the so-called non-core activities of larger European multinational (like in the automotive component supplier industry in the late 1990s), then by re-composing of the

diverse leftover industries into some kind of re-agglomerated new company structure. This movement is called "consolidation". The sole logical objective being the capacity of the owners to maximise their cash flows in the shortest possible time. Soon the new artificial MNC is sold or dissipated by either trading it back into the market (selling it to its competitor, clients, or suppliers – verticalisation) or by virtue of an IPO (Initial Public Offering), which means floating the new structured MNC on any stock exchange.

From an enterprise management point of view these "artificial" European MNCs result in mid-size MNCs of 10 000 to 40 000 employees worldwide (called "mid caps" by the investment bankers, for middle capitalisation). However, they are not coherent entities from a managerial, and most importantly, from a cultural point of view. Instead they are fragmented, with no or worse, conflicting corporate cultures and disparate national cultures (in an unmanaged way). They are the result of "assembled" blocks, which are bound to deliver an express bottom line usually within 3 years after the merger, and have to deliver an attractive business plan for a future trade sales or a compelling investor memorandum for an IPO that the "exit" strategy requires.

In terms of management there is very little integration and industrial homogeneity. R&D is mutilated and often made up of antagonist technologies. Very seldom do project pipelines of otherwise alien entities, or worse still formerly competing entities, constitute a perfect match after being merged. A typically 20 000 employee North America MNC would be a coherent entity, with coherent R&D, integrated marketing, efficient manufacturing and proficient financial reporting and control systems unlike its typical European counterpart that is most likely to be an artificial bunch of 20 or so SMEs of 1000 employees each, who may have been former competitors, grouped together, against their will under the drive of a greedy fund, with absolutely no coherence, disparate methods and systems, highly leveraged (weak own equity), with no common culture, and generalising the Tower of Babel syndrome as the rule, under a thin veil of commonality – most of the time limited to the brand new visual of identity only.

It is also likely that pan-European plants and site geographies have no logic other than multi-layers of history, stretching across Europe, with neither deep commonality in tools or systems nor any comprehensive efficient supply chains.

A typical pattern emerges when addressing the higher management echelons of these recently "re-composed" middle-sized European MNCs. Their corporate management is disparate most of the time as a result of the coagulation of the small disparate entities. It is disparate in that the company is "politically" composed, as no real culture emerges, nor prior attention has been given to leveraging on the culture diversity; the cultural diversity is a taboo factor, and consequently is not managed, and it is done in a "political" manner if and when addressed. In the executive board, or in the key task forces, or committees, one may find a Frenchman, a German, an Italian, etc., not because they are particularly competent, but because it is believed that they represent their acquired unit in France, Germany, or Italy, respectively. Mimicking the EU governance system is therefore seen as politically correct.

The result is generally either chaos or paralysis. Such a "composed" management team is bound to act using compromise by its very self-construction, when not using compromising, to avoid hurting the national unit too much; by what the pan-European corporate rationale would otherwise command, it ends in chaotic decisions or absence of decisions because it would be too painful to make any if not accepted across the board.

Mini case: Europe, the US fund and the Gordian knot

In the 1990s, an American investment group decided to invest in the then promising European automotive sector. Their strategy on paper was clear-cut and simple. It consisted of buying into several entities throughout Europe from the "debris", i.e., the non-core businesses of local groups that were engaged in other activities (such as missiles, robotics, transport systems and HVAC). In about 1 year, the US investment group acquired a myriad of about 10 units very rapidly throughout Europe (remembering "that time is money" is an American cultural trait that was discussed earlier). The price they paid for each company was not particularly fair, but since they were pressed for time that was the price to pay to "roll out" the investment program in less than a year.

They had "rolled out" a similar program in the United States within 10 months, thus they saw no reason why it be should be any different in Europe; after all, most of the fund managers knew Europe, they had all been there at least once during their holidays. However, the pace for negotiations is much slower in Europe whether in the south or in Germany. The only notable exception was the United Kingdom, where both time frame and price paid were correct, clearly because of the cultural proximity between the British sellers and the American buyers. Otherwise, each of the entities sold had a wonderful business plan dressed up, of course, ready to be executed, promising even more wonderful returns after "consolidation". To ensure that the pan-European representation was politically correct, the excessively large executive board of this new company was composed of over 20 executive members coming from the respective acquired entities. It soon became clear that moving people across Europe would be an impossible task when it came to carrying out the consolidation process by rationalising and regrouping functions, such as R&D, manufacturing, Finance and admin. This was not because the movement of people was restricted by law, but because there were many other factors involved – all culturally related that played a critical role. The American investors discovered that concentrating the R&D into one pan-European centre of excellence in Germany, of an adequate size for a now 10 000 plus employee group, would mean moving research engineers from Italy, the United Kingdom and France across Europe, where some competing R&D departments already existed. What was not considered in the equation was the fact that the vast majority of French, British and Italian engineers would not move their families, who also did not speak any foreign languages, particularly German. They would not sell their houses, apartments, etc., not to speak of the problems of finding new jobs for spouse, etc. This was something that the American investors did not have to solve when only a year earlier they had moved all the R&D engineers from all over the states into Cupertino in California. Instead the executive board of this "re-composed" European MNC typically looked for a compromise, rather than confrontation and thus opted for the very appealing concept of a virtual R&D centre. They would pool the R&D thinking power together in teams, without moving the people, using Internet combined with short and frequent travelling. The result was a disaster. Travelling expenses went soaring through the roof, and the positions of formerly competitive R&D centres did not converge by virtue of the Internet but derived into an entrenched war. The German solution started competing with French innovation, itself, of course incompatible with British developments. Why? Simply because those R&D centres were not pooled into one physical place in Europe for the formerly mentioned reasons; they were still attached to their respective national manufacturing facilities. In fact, they all knew that if a design centre would become the leader, the technology that it would have designed would become the dominant "groups" technology, de facto, imposing a one manufacturing standard, thus shedding hundreds of manufacturing jobs within their related national sites. Needless to say this R&D case was multiplied by as many functions as there were in the company. The control systems were a horrendous mix of national accounting-based reports (which we have seen how disparate or even how antagonist they can be in Europe) with a thin surface of apparently common spreadsheet and macros reporting. The executive board was geared to compromising, not to decision making, because of its heteroclite composition. As the investor policy was not to intervene in the management of their portfolio companies, there was nobody to actually cut the Gordian knot. After having lost a lot of cash mainly due to the lack of synergy that could not be effectively materialised through a pan-European consolidation and moreover the fact that each national entity became destabilised, the American investment group decided to sell this now ailing business to a first-tier automotive supplier at a price much lower than the one they initially paid for. The automotive supplier proceeded to break this composite incoherent and unmanageable group back into their national components and integrate the most potentially profitable parts into its large national entities. They cut the Gordon knot, and solved the case, at least for a while. This large European automotive company was itself, under pressure, in 2007, from another very large US investment fund forcing it to consolidate with another US-based, and of course, competing automotive supplier in which it had invested with the intent of delivering wonderful future synergic returns after an obvious "on paper consolidation" – déjà vu.

In other words, there is no European model per se. Europe is intrinsically characterised by diversity and fragmentation contrary to the uniformed United States, after all their constituents have been melted into one single metal via the melting pot: e pluribus unum. However, diversity is not a problem, and even less of a problem to solve as it is encrypted forever in Europe DNA. Successful management and controlling in Europe requires managing not against cultures but across and with cultures. The four main patterns have been seen and discussed earlier. In contrast to the United States, managing and controlling in Europe requires a great deal of attention to cultures, preferably in an ex ante way; and particularly attention should be brought to adequately balance corporate and national cultures.

6.3.3 The complex interfaces/configurations: Joint ventures, Networks, aliances

It is very frequent to establish some "softer" forms of co-operations between different parties in international business. They can vary from the hard–soft forms (e.g., joint ventures) to soft–soft forms (e.g., networks or alliances).

In the majority of cases a joint venture is catechised by a form of co-operation as a result of a legal entity, where two or more "partners" co-invest in a project. The investment of each party can vary in nature, or size. For example, a French cosmetic manufacturer may want to joint venture with a Chinese distributor to manufacture and market cosmetics in China, where the French manufacturer would contribute its IP (licenses). The Chinese distributor would contribute its national distribution network, and each partner would input 5 million euros into a China-based manufacturing facility.

Here, we have a clear-cut project and an adequate structure to house the project: the joint venture.

Controlling a joint venture is not easy. This is because the controller – the managing director and the managing team – must be very clear that they are acting for the sole benefit of the joint venture and not its constituting partners. Although it may look the same it is certainly not.

Mini case: When South/South equals Win/Win

The author was chartered by the president of a major US composite and technology glass corporation, as his "special envoy", to try to unlock a difficult situation that had developed in a South African company. This large American Corporation had entered into a joint venture a few years ago with a local manufacturing company which had five composite and fibre plants in South Africa. Everything was going smoothly, until recently when a major conflict started among the local South African shareholders that had formally escalated, via lawyers, to the higher echelon of the Illinois worldwide HQ in the United States. Moreover the local managing director, a German national expatriated from the American shareholding partner group, was under no less that nine law suits filed in the Johannesburg court, among which were corruption, untruthful management and insider trading, and he was under personal investigation. Needless to say that the situation was serious enough to understand that fast action was actually required to remedy it. After decades of enjoying a market share in the range of 65–70%, the South African joint venture had brutally fallen to a 35–40% market position in less than 6 months. Its cash flow swung from an all time positive 60 million rand to a negative 80 million, and a severe strike was paralysing the 5 plants. A few months ago, the CEO's position in the joint venture had been occupied by a senior local manager who retired at the age of 65 after having served his entire career with the local industry. It had now been filled up by a young expatriate, who came from the US group. He was a German national and his background was research. He was in fact the R&D director of a US plant from which he had been recently promoted due to the excellent quality of his work on composite tiles in the aerospace application for the shuttle. This new role as CEO was intended to be a reward for him and seen from the HQ as being an "easy and relax" 3 year assignment intended to be just a launch pad for a high flyer before orbiting in the highest corporate constellations on his way out of Africa – in 3 years time. During his first 2 months of office, he had made a series of fatal decisions without consulting his board. He had decided to outsource the distribution of all the products and thus to operate via a distributor – to which the joint venture's business represented less than 2% of the distributor's total turnover – under the rationale that distributing costs would be less if outsourced than if owned. The decision was made by a major international consulting firm, the leading partner of which was also a German, a "Doktor" from the same German Engineering University, who was in charge of the project. This decision immediately provoked a sharp drop in the market share, as the distributor had no direct interest in pushing the products; and at its best, no more than 2% of its capacity. Under the same influence, the newly appointed CEO decided that he would let the distributor have a free 6 months credit to pay for the purchases of finished goods to help him in the transition and make 2 months of sales inventory available to him at the joint venture's cost (a sort of bonded warehouse). Cash flow thus plummeted: turnover almost halved and no cash flowed in for above 8 months. It was a lethal set of self-made (perceived as) arrogant decisions. In his drive for cost cutting he implemented a brand new and extremely costly comprehensive information system which was meant to replace the former cost accounting system which, in passing, was altering the fixed cost allocations with the result of changing the profitability structure of all product ranges. This is because it was the exact replication of the German software that he was used to running in Germany. He only perceived the cybernetic dimension not realising that by the same token he was changing the fundamental accounting rules, which required not only a board of director's agreement, but a general assembly meeting with an auditor's opinion on the fairness, a memorandum to shareholders. The final factor that ultimately triggered the local shareholders to rebel was the fact that a smart local plant manager had managed to get the joint venture successfully shortlisted for a tender on a large project, in South America, regarding rock wool which would likely recur and thus cope with the ailing domestic market share – a disease the German CEO had self-inflicted to the otherwise healthy joint venture, This entrepreneurial local manager had fostered a secure market, with low shipment costs at a good margin, a good export business for the South African joint venture especially in those days of meagre cows. However, the joint venture CEO discussed it with a divisional head within the American HQ who he still believed was his management and where his loyalty still laid and where his career prospects were after the African assignment. Unfortunately, it so happened that this US divisional head was interested to penetrate this business directly from the US corporation, at a slightly inferior price and by doing so they would not have to divide the profit in two with the South Africans.

This example shows a typical case of how complex management of a joint venture can be: a typical conflict of interests and loyalties of management arises. Although the intent of the joint venture CEO was not personal enrichment, his future career prospects could be analysed as such; he was clearly depleting the substance of the joint venture in favour of one of the shareholder only. This German CEO just forgot that he was the joint venture's CEO and that he had to act for the best interest of the joint venture and not one of his partners. With the management team, and both shareholders, the lost confidence was restored, the conflicts diffused and the business model rebuilt. The joint venture was flourishing again a year later and the cash flow was positive once again. The South African/South American export business developed nicely into a win-win deal that lasts even today; but more importantly, smiles were back on all faces. Under the author's recommendations the entrepreneurial local plant manager was made CEO, and the German rocket science "Doktor" slipped off the radar screen after he left the group, where once he thought his future lay.

Controlling the case of a joint venture implies a true and clear understanding that the joint venture is a distinct entity when compared to its respective partners. This is easier said than done because things may be entangled on the field.

Other forms of co-operations are even more difficult to manage and control because they are more elusive. This is the case for networks or alliances. Alliances and networks mostly fluctuate over time and are not housed within a legal, clear-cut entity. It can range from a series of formally mutually binding agreements like the one binding a principal to its agent, or the code share flights, or franchising systems, or pools of interests like the pools grouping air carriers together, hotels chains and car renters into apparently comprehensive frequent traveller's fidelity programmes.

It can also be more elusive like think tanks, circles of influence, including lobbies and NGOs or just loose and non-visible connections.

This latter aspect can be the dark side of alliances or networks, which may be conducive to oligopolies, undeclared cartels or distorted free market conditions – even corruption in the Western sense.

Needless to say that control mechanisms might neither be easy nor welcomed.

In other words, managing and controlling international joint ventures, alliances and networks not only require technical and managerial competence but an acute sense of cultural awareness as well.

6.4 The M&As

International Mergers and Acquisitions (M&As) consistently and constantly fail.

All surveys carried out over the past 15 years from academia and consulting industries alike come to the same conclusion: between 75% and 85% of international M&As fail.

Kearney (2004), Coopers & Lybrand which became Price Waterhouse Corporation in 1992, Demeure (2000), Habeck et al. (2001), Chaterjee et al. (1992), (Guth, 1998), Mayhofer (2001), Batchelder (1993), Meier (2001), Adler (2004), Kent (2003), Amon (1989), Hofstede, IMD and INSEAD Professor (2001), Sudi Sudarsanam, Cranfield Business School Professor(2003), Towers Perin International Human Resource Consulting.

The parties are worse off after the merger than before and failure is most likely to occur in the first 3 years after inception. The causes are systematically identified as being the same; they all root back to cultural issues such as antagonist national cultures, inadequate product offering to local markets, organisational structure at odds with national values and beliefs, integration not performed and management styles that are incompatible.

Very seldom are the so-called "hard factors" such as technology or finance found as the root causes.

By just looking at the facts, it is striking to see that large and reputable M&A companies have blatantly failed: DaimlerChrysler, Hoechst-Rhone Poulenc Rorer, Alcatel-Lucent, Electrowatt–Landis & Gyr and Sabena-Swissair-AOM are amongst the few.

No one would think that they had not carefully screened the pros and cons beforehand in exactly the same way as they did before launching so many products or projects that have made them so successful in the past. One can also be assured that they obtained all the necessary support from expert worldwide consulting firms, be it lawyers, strategy consultants, operations consultants, accountants, due diligence specialists, investment bankers and valuators economists, brand consultants, IP consultants, communications consultants, HR consultants, etc., and despite this it almost invariably fails.

Why? Because cultural issues are never dealt with ex ante and very seldom ex post.

Mini case: International M&As would be a lot simpler if only they were just domestic

Very recently when it came to the attention of the author that a merger of equals was decided between a major and very emblematic US originating high-tech corporation and a very visible and emblematic French corporation, the author decided to contact the CEO of the American corporation as he "sensed" that this manager would become the big boss of the merged entity to help her out on managing the cultural dimensions ex ante in this very risky venture for all stakeholders' sake. She very kindly and immediately answered that the integration was in her view a non-issue, and furthermore she had everything "under control". The author was a bit surprised because although she was probably an excellent businessperson, nowhere had she had personal experience of expatriation and particular dealings with the French business world and French management style. He wondered how she was going to do? His curiosity did not have to last for long. Not even a year after the finalisation of the merger, the new corporations after joining with the two century old high-tech companies which have weathered many storms, including two world wars, was on the verge of bankruptcy, and at the last extraordinary shareholder meeting, the share price having fallen constantly, she got almost fired; but, in extremis, saved her head this time by deflecting the blow onto her deputy who she fired on the spot (the deputy was given a very heavy pay cheque nevertheless). In the meantime, more than 20 000 employees had lost their jobs on both sides of the Atlantic, contributing to the so-called "synergy" that failed to materialised. The author felt sorry for the workers, both side of the Atlantic and elsewhere in the world, as well as for the shareholders, since it was clear right from the beginning that their cultures were at odds with each other. (How to diagnose, make cultural clashes prognosis and to bridge gaps and leverages on differences for a sustained outstanding performance will be discussed in more detail in Chapter 8).

This case is unfortunately the general rule, not the exception.

The legitimate question is why is this cultural aspect not seriously taken into consideration as being not only a success determinant but also a prime determinant if that is the case?

There are two direct answers to this, which comes back to the main drivers that command an M&A:

(1) Ego
(2) Greed and lust.

Ego is what compels the CEO and/or the board members who drive the merger and lead the charge. Even when it is presented as a merger of equals, mechanically the acquiring CEO's ego just doubles – more than that, the CEO enters into the company's history; This exhilarating feeling is very powerful since it deals with hormones before neurones, and like other very powerful hormone-driven stimuli, they are almost impossible to control, although the strategies and tactics deployed to grasp the "reward" can be intensively "neuronal", thus sophisticated. This is the classical Alexander the Great quest for more conquests syndrome, a never-ending need for more adrenaline, leading to conquer more land than he could ever control or use. After his death, the lands he had conquered were not better off, but worse off: after the M&A climax, the shares almost invariably collapse. The same happened with Attila or Genghis Kahn or Napoleon, etc.; the situation they left was much worse by all standards. That is THE driver, nothing more complicated since the dawn of mankind, where during those days the winning tribe members of an M&A team (murder & acquisition) used to eat the brains of the losers to display their superiority. Winner takes everything as a rule. It still is the case today, in the majority of cases. Prestigious MBAs and 3G Internet laptops and PDAs and elaborate press communiqués do not change the classical core of the epics; they just update the costumes and lyrics.

Greed and lust are the other determinants. M&As always make the shares rise before they fall flat on their face after the failure. But in between these two events there is window of time to make easy money heaps of money, even billions. Banks and traders are excellent at the game, they are not ego-driven; they are just greed-driven. Then comes the cohort of expensive international lawyers, consultants, auditors accountants, communication gurus, brand specialist, etc. Each M&A is a feast. Thousands, hundreds of thousands of hours billed. The more and bigger the M&A the better it is.

Incidentally, on the subject of greed, the failed CEOs usually make more money than when they do through succeeding, by virtue of golden parachutes (big pay offs) and stock options that they were given before the anticlimax. This practice has given rise, recently, to much investigation by the stock exchange control authorities, but real action is still scarce especially in Europe where class actions and proxy hunting do not exist. Strictly speaking from a purely "scientific" point of view, it would mean that out of four international M&As, three are bound to be failures, with their associated trail of job destruction and value destruction if the very short speculative window of time at the stock exchange is accepted.

This is never addressed in business plans or merger memoranda.

Here there is a real control issue, entangled within an even more serious corporate governance issue. It is amazing to see that there are inevitably only benefits in projected business plans, post-merger integrations consequences, "synergies", etc., when it is a clear scientific fact that statistically in the vast majority of cases the opposite will happen. It is surprising to say the least that there is no formal compulsory section in all M&A memoranda discussing the reasons why the considered and proposed deal to the shareholders will not be a failure this time, and how the cultural issues are specifically addressed by management.

Out of the 75% failure rate 20–30% could turn into success by not only careful attention and not ignoring the cultural factors, as is done today, but by also addressing them and managing them either ex ante (up front) which is the best way, or ex post (after the fact) which is a less preferred but better than nothing.

It remains a fact that a significant portion of international M&As deals should never take place, provided the cultural dimensions would be part (and on top) of the due diligence process since those very cultural factors are the root causes of the too often subsequent failures.

The subject of how this can be orchestrated will be discussed in more detail in Chapter 8.

Summary

Cultural factors are the prime dimension in complex international business development; at the moment it implies cultural interfaces – every time a border is crossed, which means all the time. It means that cultural differences do exist and that they will not disappear by some kind of "convergence". On the contrary, one only needs to look around on the worldwide political scene to understand that the cultural dimensions are everywhere, no less than before, but much more than before the fall of the so-called iron curtain. And they will be so forever.

The world is not flat, never has it been and never will it be.

The history of mankind is full of attempts to flatten the world, all have blatantly failed, most of the time resulting in bloodshed.

Consequently, cultural differences are not an obstacle to dodge, bulldozer out, blow up, roll over, avoid, or hide. Cultural differences are not part of the problem; they are part of the solution. Cultural differences are not a subject of study for the19th century anthropologists; it is a subject for 21st century managers – a subject for action.

At the beginning of this chapter it was seen how varied Europe is.

But Asia is equally varied. There is very little in common between Chinese, Koreans, Vietnamese, Indians, Mongols, Japanese, Afghans, Indonesians and Turks. They are all people living in Asia, be it eastern Asia, Southeast Asia, sub-continental Asia, central Asia, islands in Asia or Asia Minor. They completely differ; they had been at war with each other almost continuously for centuries (exactly like the people of Europe who have been at war continuously with each other culminating with the 20th century when Europe decided to commit suicide twice in less than 30 years).

The Pacific Rim is also extremely diverse. In contrast to classical North American MNC's arbitrary marketing segmentation is the Asia Pacific Region, where they lump the Asia and the Pacific together into one "region" (which is already better than the "rest of the world"). Moreover the Pacific as a region is immense, extremely varied and fragmented, with many cultures in their own rights co-existing, not to speak of the immense variety of languages.

The uniform or more precisely the uniformed culture of the United States is actually an exception rather than a rule in the world. And even this is changing, referring to the Hispanic, African and Asiatic originating cultures, the self-expression and affirmation of which is growing inside the United States.

Cultural differences are not the problems that will drag a company behind; they are the resources that should be used to leverage to single the company out on the market place, because a market is a place where people buy from people, not where machines exchange code lines with other machines.

Love and nurture and respect cultural differences, they will pay off centuple times over.

M&As are unfortunately the perfect example where cultural differences are never part of the equation. Has anyone ever seen a DFC (Discounted Cash Flow) model factoring in the cultural variables? The sanctions are clear: above 75% of international M&As are fiascos, destroying jobs and shareholder's values alike. Although for the share flippers and consultants, it might be an instant bonanza. This poses a serious problem towards the capability of controlling concepts, models and tools such as DFC, comparable and multiples, due diligence, and financial audits, which fail to capture the scope of the issue and fall short of giving a fair assessment of the sustainability of a firm by failing to put in the first place the aspect that should be assessed first, i.e., the cultural dimension.

It also poses a very serious corporate governance issue, which so far remains unaddressed in a commensurate manner.

References

Adler, L. (2004), *International Dimensions of Organisational Behaviour.*
Amon, A. (1989), Marketing Management 12.
Batchelder, W. (1993), The International Marketing.
Chaterjee, et al. (1992), *The Harvard Business Review* 4.
Demeure, G. (2000), *The Economist Intelligence Unit.*
Guth, H. (1998), *Proceedings of Management.*
Habeck, H. et al. (2001), *The Economist Intelligence Unit.*
Hegel, G. (1817), *Encyclopaedia der philopspphischen wissenschaften in grundrisse.*
Hofstede, G. (2001), *Culture Consequences.*
Kearney, A.T. (2004), *Strategy and Leadership* 32, No. 2.
Kent, P. (2003), *International Business Review* 4.
Marx, K. (1867), Das Kapital.
Mayhofer, J. (2001), *Les cahiers du Managements.*
Meier, F. (2001), *Banque et Finance.*
Sudarsanam, S. (2003), *Creating Value for Mergers and Acquisitions.*

Which profile for which type of international business controller?

This chapter is aimed at trying to clarify the respective roles, functions and "qualities" attached to classical controlling positions. The roles and functions have been arbitrarily segmented into five main areas:

(1) The international HQ group Controller
(2) The international trading resale subsidiary controller
(3) The international manufacturing subsidiary controller
(4) The international joint venture controller
(5) The international project controller.

The reason behind this a priori segmentation is to make the distinction and description easier although contours of functions in reality may well of course not be so clear-cut. For the sake of clarity, a "job profile" format has been adopted that is concise although looking a bit abrupt.

7.1 The international HQ Group Controller

7.1.1 Role

The international HQ group controller performs the ultimate controlling function in the organisation. The international HQ group controller has a triple responsibility:

Ensures a seamless consolidation of all the group's data and information to help make informed and sound management decisions. Thus special care is given to the data integrity and consistency throughout the group emanating from the maze of subsidiaries, affiliates, etc. Special attention must be given to off balance sheet elements and consolidation perimeter (off shore entities). Since the international HQ Group Controller is an executive board (EB) member of the group, the controller must make sure that a comprehensive and in-depth understanding of economics and financial drivers is achieved in a timely and accurate manner, that is, by segment of businesses, regions, market, organisation, projects, etc., and undistorted by the tax driven intra-group transfer prices. The latter point requires a strong cost accounting system.

Ensures a compliant and informative reporting to the outside stakeholders.

Be in a position to pro-actively propose scenarios and action plans to his EB colleagues, as well as evaluate policies, strategies, investments, programs and projects. The treasury and equity management may or may not be part of the role according to different organisations.

7.1.2 Reporting lines

The reporting lines are towards the group CEO, or as an alternative towards the group CFO, if that position co-exists with that of the controller.

For subsidiaries, regions, projects, etc., the controller may or may not report via a solid line (meaning hierarchically) to the international HQ Group Controller. They may also report via dotted line (meaning only functionally).

This is not a matter of detail but it is an important point. No solution is a priori better than the other. The important point is that whichever way is chosen, it must be in harmony with the corporate culture and the national culture.

The solid line option gives a very strong weight to the finance function throughout the organisation. The finance community is thus a "state within a state". This gives more coherence to the controlling and also ensures a real independence for the controllers vis à vis their bosses or colleagues, thus giving a great level of impartiality to figures and information. However, on the negative side, a distance is often created between the local controllers and their colleagues and the boss, resulting in a low team spirit.

Taken to the extreme, the solid reporting line may create the "NSA" (National Security Agency) type of syndrome and related trauma to the whole enterprise. It is interesting to note that the new generations of ERPs (Enterprise Resources Planning) are mimicking the NSA "surveillance" systems in "spirit" and even their selling argument is that these ERPs make it technologically possible to introduce a permanent "spy" type of culture in enterprises.

Mini case: Soax and the European precedents

Following high visibility scandals affecting US corporations like Enron, WorldCom, Arthur Andersen and the like, the US government has recently, under pressure, passed an act that was supposed to eradicate such malpractice forever. Among the battery of regulations, two are worth looking from a cultural point of view.

Firstly, "whistle blowing". This allows *anyone* who may *only suspect* a colleague or superior of doing something wrong to and *must, under cover of anonymity*, denounce that person (most of the time by mean of an anonymous "hotline") to a special investigation bureau. The reason the authorities give is to encourage employees to speak up and stop malpractice, corruption, etc. This "culture" and "procedure" is not new. It has existed for centuries and has proved to be a very popular and efficient system to crunch practices that were non-compliant with the governing rules. It was put into place very effectively by Himmler's Gestapo during the Nazi period of occupation in France, Holland, Norway, Poland, etc., in World War II where unfortunately millions of people, who only needed to be suspected by "colleagues" or "neighbours" for not complying to the new regime, were denounced to the Kommandantur mostly out of jealousy or greed for obtaining a vacant property under the comfortable cover of anonymity, and from then on sent to the "camps" from where most of them never returned. A similar practice was used by the KGB during the communist period in the USSR to a far greater devastating effect where no less than 30 million were killed under Saline's regime and afterwards. The combination of presumption, denunciation, anonymity, constant mutual "surveillance" worked then to its full extent in the populace but with adverse effects as we now know. Implementing Sarbanes–Oxley Act in some European countries and imposing anonymous denunciation as a sign of progress and higher ethics is at best a sign of gross ignorance, and in most cases resented as provocation, arrogance and humiliation vis à vis those who suffered from the similar practice in times before.

Secondly, it was recently forbidden for audit firms in the United States to have consulting or advisory services under one roof simultaneously. This led to a (pro forma) split up of the big four and inter alia in different legal entities avoid conflicts of interest: auditors may sometimes be tempted to turn a blind eye on an otherwise ailing business just to prolong a lucrative consulting mandate with the firm, engaged with the legal consulting practice arm of the same firm.

In France this situation of conflict of interests could never occur as it has always been the law that the audit (le chiffre) and the legal/tax advice (le droit) remain separate. Interestingly, French auditors and lawyers, who were adamant in keeping their status quo, were systematically criticised by their US counterparts as being old fashioned, until Soax made it "cool".

Beyond the national cultures that profoundly affect the board of directors' role, the radical change in corporate ownership that occurred as a tidal wave over the past years has affected its relation to power and the stakeholders. This has been the case because as much as 66% of shares were in the hands of institutional funds in 2005.

This brings us immediately to the question of the board of directors' role and its capacity to balance corporate decisions as per the UN encouraged triple bottom line approach: social, environmental and economical, which is also embodied in the "Global Compact".

7.1.3 Background

As seen in the former chapters, the background understandably varies according to countries and cultures. In most cases an MBA, CA, CPA background will be necessary because technical content is high, coupled with a large experience in international business, namely, transfer prices and foreign exchange (FX) and consolidation processes.

A former business experience is often an added advantage.

7.1.4 Cross-cultural qualities

The level of interface with different cultures is important but not intense. Interfacing is mostly limited to local controllers reporting to the international HQ Group Controller, thus there is exposure but it is not overwhelming. However, former assignments as either subsidiary controller or an international project manager is a prerequisite. Understanding and fitting into corporate culture is a key element of the job, as well as the capacity to interact with external stakeholders. A sound business sense is also important.

7.2 The international resale trading subsidiary controller

7.2.1 Role

The main role of an international resale trading subsidiary controller is to maintain the trading subsidiary in synchronisation with its own function, i.e., to distribute goods imported from within the group, and to maintain an adequate local tax compliant profit margin, in general, by international standards in the range of 2–4% of sales. In the same vein, and in line with the discussions in Chapter 3, the controller must keep the assets and the costs under control on which he/she has a lever, that is, accounts receivables, inventories, other working capital constituents, and administrative costs.

7.2.2 Reporting lines

The subsidiary controller reports hierarchically to the resale trading subsidiary CEO and functionally to the international HQ Group Controller or vice versa.

The discussion is the same with its respective pros and cons.

The question is whether the international resale trading subsidiary controller should be an expatriate or a local recruit.

Again this is not a neutral choice. In the case where an expatriate is chosen from the parent company and added to this if the expatriate reports directly to the group controller, instead of choosing a local national as the subsidiary CEO, the message sent out is clear: the group does not totally trust the local team or believe that locals are not competent enough or both. It does not mean that this will not work. It just carries a strong message. It was very common for US MNCs to operate this way until the mid-90s.

Taking this option risks leaving a bad taste in the long run.

7.2.3 Background

The level of complexity requested by the position is low. It might be complicated because of the numbers of products, divisions, etc., but in essence it remains simple.

The background is consequently less demanding and an accounting background or bachelor level in economics should in most cases suffice. However, preparation of local statutory reports and tax returns, as well as regularly and timely reporting to the parent company requires a good level of proficiency in local and group GAAPs.

7.2.4 Cross-cultural qualities

The position is highly exposed to a cultural interface among the local market, local authorities, the local organisation and colleagues, local stakeholders, and the parent company.

Possessing cultural capabilities is paramount, and this must be taken into account when profiling such a function. The more the local controller is able to capture, decode, analyse and process information signals on a large and adequate cultural broadband the better it is for monitoring the business. Let us always bear in mind that 97% of information is not formatted in quantitative data, but it is floating around as qualitative inputs. Without prejudging whether the subsidiary controller should or should not be a local national, since this is a group policy and corporate cultural decision as stated earlier, it is however clear that the local controller must be extremely proficient in the local culture, if bicultural, when expatriate. All the more so when the subsidiary is located in nations where the culture is implicit, of low context, collectivist and with a low PDI (Power Distance Index), i.e., the vast majorities of countries in the world, including the so-called emerging economies.

7.3 The international manufacturing subsidiary controller

7.3.1 Role

The role of the controller of an international manufacturing subsidiary is one of the most difficult positions along with that of an international joint venture and international project controller's position.

To ensure that the business is performing at its best, the controller along with the other subsidiary EB members must contribute to monitoring. The business in question must possess at least one manufacturing facility, if not several other potentially various outsourced manufacturing processes, plus a substantial comprehensive supply chain, with inbound and outbound loops.

The international manufacturing subsidiary controller has many more levers on his hands than the resale trading subsidiary controller. The control spans on virtually 100% of the value added which is locally produced, with the minor exception of management and intellectual property (IP)–related fees from parent companies and the like.

Monitoring of raw materials requires a permanent surveillance as to whether it is sourced locally or externally, or from the parent company depending on a myriad of usually conflicting factors such as parent company's big picture economics, local raw material prices, customs and duties on import and FX coverage.

Energy and utilities are less of a problem as most production processes require that they are sourced locally, otherwise it would prove physically impractical or counter-productive.

The same is the case with labour. Unless specialised expertise cannot be sourced locally, the labour force should always be local due to costs reasons. In most cases this is normally the reason for having created a foreign subsidiary in the first place.

Local selling prices also have to be monitored, but the role of the international subsidiary controller does not differ from that of the international trading subsidiary here. It differs when part of the local production is resold to the group's entities, or directly to the parent company, or through an off shore trading vehicle, or even to another group production unit for further development (component of a whole). This requires very fine tuning and dynamic monitoring, as trends and cycles are typically not in synchronisation with each other, not forgetting of course the inner production cycle including the whole supply chain cycle.

Depending on the aforementioned, FX is also much more sophisticated at this level. It requires a real-time monitoring and series of projection models linked to all cycles and their relative exposures in multicurrencies. Inertia in working capital FX (especially receivables, inventories, work in process, and payables and the related currencies in which they are denominated), and working capital cycles (time and amplitude) requires careful monitoring and controlling.

Mini case: When the Group is wrong and the subsidiary is right

Subsidiary Controller versus Room Controller

A few years ago, the author was appointed managing director to the UK engineering, manufacturing and marketing subsidiary of a very well-known Swiss international high-tech group, which had 50 000 employees worldwide, manufacturing and marketing, inter alia, HVAC (heating, ventilation, air conditioning), telecoms, energy management and security systems. The UK subsidiary was in a critical state as they were consistently and constantly loosing around £5 to £10 million per year over the past several years. The author was appointed to get the company back on track once and for all. To start with, the morale was low; employees expecting more pain from market and hits from the parent company. The pressure was paramount with an obligation to succeed and any decision that had to be made had to be fast and right to the point as too many mistakes had been made over the years to allow for any wrong choices again. Just one guideline was given to all the employees by the author on his first day in office: "No taboos! Make any suggestions that were thought to be adequate". The root causes were found to be multiple and too long and complicated to list in this book. However one of the causes in this parent/international subsidiary context is worth mentioning. One of the HVAC technologies was a superb room temperature gauge controller that allowed fantastic possibilities from a pure technological point of view (a room controller monitors the temperature, air humidity and even the access security levels of a room). However, this room controller was engineered in Switzerland by highly technical personnel and initially designed for markets where customers were rich (one of the highest income per capita in the world) and where technology is a matter of national pride (Swiss quality).

The UK market was responding to very different economic and socio-logical drivers: the customers were extremely price-sensitive (the lower the price the bigger the market share, and conversely, the higher the price, no sales, regardless of the above average technological performance) and technologically unaware. Simple and robust commands were enough, therefore there was no need to have temperature controls to a precise quarter of a Celsius degree, with daily cycles, weekly cycles and yearly cycle programming, topped with the possibilities of remote distance control for abroad in case the person has a 3 hour delayed overseas flight and did not need their particular London apartment to be overheated when arriving! A rapid solution was found using the local team to make a low cost/local market adapted room control temperature gauge to sell into the market for today's needs. It was estimated that almost half of the subsidiary's losses could be recuperated. This actually turned out to be only one third as the situation was proved to be more corrupted than expected by other aspects, which were subsequently corrected in less than a year. It was calculated that a 40% cost decrease was necessary. And this was needed for yesterday. However, at that moment the Swiss parent manufacturing and R&D team heavily objected to this decision. Naturally they were aware of the problem, although not in minute detail, but for them there was no question of change. They upheld that their technology was superior and as it was the group's technology they were right and it was rather the UK customer who was not up to the level of their technology. It was esteemed that the UK consumer had to be "educated" to their "Swiss-made" marvels. However, the UK end user was not the decision maker, because the market was driven by UK contractors building merchants and consultants – all of whom had their own purchasing drivers, and superior quality with high price was just not on their list. The parent company was wrong all the way. The parent company's economic equation coupled with some R&D and manufacturing manager's egos was detrimental to the business. Pushing pallets full of overengineered Swiss-made temperature controllers in the UK warehouses, where they would either quietly wait for 3 years before being written off or eventually sold for a large discount, creating a 40% loss was going to help no one neither the UK subsidiary nor the parent company, and especially not the group worldwide. After a fierce discussion took place ending with room temperature gauge controllers being designed using simpler electronic logics, with a substantially improved consumer man–machine interface, 3 pushes to set the controls instead of the previous 12 were manufactured and shipped from China for an all inclusive 38% lesser cost. The story has a happy ending: This UK example interested other colleagues and managing directors elsewhere in Europe and in the United States who were also suffering from the same parent company "push" syndrome on the same product line (Germany was all right, but even the United States was having trouble selling the product with a positive margin). Ultimately, the Chinese off shore supplier became the worldwide group's supplier, and the super-sophisticated Swiss-made room controller was redirected towards higher-end engineering markets such as hospital operating theatres, laboratories, semi-conductor factories and white rooms facilities, where sophisticated temperature and room controls were important and where it obtained full acceptance and success.

The author's controller and her team were proud to have made a wonderful economic and business analysis that helped not only resurrect the UK company but also prove that thinking laterally pays off. The profound understanding of the UK culture in terms of attitude towards price versus perceived technology was a key driver in the turnaround, in line with her technical skills and her team's political incorrectness (also called courage) to challenge a dogma from the parent company. In this context, the "no taboo motto" paid off hundred more times than political conformity.

7.3.2   Reporting lines

It is same as in the former examples. The controller can either report hierarchically to the local CEO and functionally to the group HQ group controller situated in the parent company, or vice versa.

Again, the configuration is far from being neutral, having the same connotations as discussed earlier.

The employee may be a local national or an expatriate, and invariable the combination; expatriate and reporting hierarchically to the HQ group controller, sends the same and always strong message to the subsidiary and local community: we, the group either do not trust you (enough) and/or we, the group, believe you are not competent (enough), so have to put our own man/woman in there. There are pros and cons which ultimately come back to a cultural dimension (corporate culture and parent national culture) beyond the cost/benefit or the perceived cost/benefit of such a decision.

7.3.3 Background

The background must be very strong as this is one of the most difficult positions to hold.

The person must be technically impeccable (from Latin without "pecata", meaning literally without "sins") in terms of business and economic and financial analysis skills. This would need someone from an MBA and or accountancy background.

The production and R&D contents would also need someone with an engineering background as well, because it would help grasp the industrial, engineering and designing challenges and complexities, especially if sequences of the processes are to be outsourced or off shored.

Experience in human relation and communication skills is paramount: capacity to interact at all levels from shop floor to the board room level in tense and difficult times as well as relaxed times too.

7.3.4 Cross-cultural qualities

Being able to interface between local realities, cultural dimensions, values, rituals, societal beliefs and the corporate values, organisational cultures, and the parent company's home culture is a key factor of success for the controller, the subsidiary and the group. Such a role should never been given on the basis of technical expertise only. Experience says that this would be a recipe for failure. Based on extensive international business-controlling experience, the best split for the employee to be successful would be to have two-third proven skills in cross-culture and one-third solid technical skills coupled with a robust sense of humour, starting with the capability of laughing at oneself, as well as proving a degree of maturity and humility, which are definitely needed.

7.4 The international joint venture controller

7.4.1 Role

This is probably if not one of the, most difficult role as a controller. As discussed in Chapter 6, joint ventures pose the immediate question of interfacing cultures and managing conflict of interests. Controlling such an entity is not an easy straightforward task. With few exceptions to the rules, joint ventures are ventures made between parties who would otherwise have antagonistic interests, such as a manufacturer and a distributor, as in our earlier case between the French cosmetics manufacturer and the Chinese distributor. The conflict is on sharing the margin in the fairest way possible. The natural temptation of the manufacturer in the joint venture is to maximise its income via the joint venture through the value-added chain, by virtue of verticalisation. Naturally the manufacturer is tempted to make overstated manufacturing costs that already contain a hidden element of profit for himself alone, before sharing it with the partner, being the distributor in this case. Or the joint venturers, otherwise normally competitors, may decide to share a common distribution network in Korea, e.g., to minimise structural costs. In this case it would be natural for each partner to want to out market its other partner who otherwise would be its competitor, despite the fact that they share some of the same infrastructure in the joint venture. Despite being very frequent, these are naturally only simplistic situations chosen for the sake of exemplifying the constant conflict of interests and the controller's need to do a balancing act.

The controller's role is to monitor, control and guide management in the best possible way and in the joint venture's best interests and certainly not for any particular individual partner/shareholder's interest. In practice, and very often in reality, this means that the controller will have to ensure that firstly he/she has a firm grip on the inner economics and financials of the joint venture even if the accounting and treasury is performed by or based on the partner's group entity systems. Secondly, he/she does not report hierarchically to either of the partner's group's controllers. Thirdly, he/she understands the joint venture's business model in details.

Mini case: The US multinational, and its nationalised joint venture. What do you aim for today Mister Chairman, Cash or Profit?

Having been extensively trained in the US HQ on the East Coast and having worked in a super efficient petrochemical complex in Texas, a young graduate from an European school of management had just been assigned a brand new investment of almost a billion US dollars, that had just been made a joint venture on a 50/50 basis with a major French petrochemical group. The deal was simple on paper. It was agreed that the Americans would bring the whole IP, and the French the site and labour. Both would put in the necessary cash investment of 50/50. It appeared to be as simple as 123. Theoretically, it was supposed to be an easy ride, not lazy, but easy. The joint venture complex was the clone replica of the Texas complex; where the young graduate used to work as a trainee. He knew this plant inside out; the cost of materials, the routings, the yields, the reporting and controlling systems, the dollar per ton for raw materials costs; so much so that he could almost "sense" the complex. He could hear it breathe, and knew when it would cough (miss the budget) before it did or if was going to, and if it had fever (over use of materials), etc. He was prepared. The first months went like a dream. His French and American colleagues were working in harmony, the only notable incident occurred at the inauguration of this mega and technology-advanced complex. The American team had decided for a surprise; they organised a mega barbecue the Texan way of course. It was a pure delight. However, to be a real Texan they had imported tons of Texan beef (whole carcasses) flown in directly from Austin, in Texas. This was not taken well by all French participants, as some of them felt insulted in that the Texans could think that France, being the second largest agricultural power in the world could not produce good enough meat to meet the Texan standards. Fortunately after every one had tasted the barbecues, the dispute naturally, if not, totally settled, or at least soothed away. The cans of beer finished the appeasement job properly. A few months after our hero had started his assignment, France went through a presidential election and a socialist president was elected for based on large

Communist backing and the large Socialist majority in parliament took office. Immediately the new president decided to apply his electoral promises to the letter. Among the 101 promises, one was to nationalise all large French MNCs in strategic sectors. Petrochemicals were part of it and the French partner in the joint venture was first on the list. The French parent partner company was delisted from the stock exchange within days and became a stated-owned company. As simple as that in this French democracy, the Americans learnt that day! It was just the exact repeat scenario of what had happened to their other major petrochemical complex that they had in Iran the year before. A brand new multimillion dollar refinery had just been "nationalised" overnight in the same way and had become the property of the Iranian state – an interesting context. At 27 years of age he, the author actually, became the controller of a joint venture overnight, where 50% of the shareholders were American MNC whilst the other 50% were the property of the French state. The joint venture performed extremely well in its first fiscal year, technically, economically and financially. The market was booming (it was before the dollar/French franc parity collapsed and made the entire purpose of the project of producing in France pointless as opposed to importing from the United States, unlike before the investment, but this has already been discussed in a former chapter). The result was the generation of a hefty EBIT DA. "The" question came at a board meeting. The communist French state commissioner wanted to demonstrate to the French business community and the public that Communists and Socialists were able to govern corporations together seriously; thanks to employee's devotion. They considered that they could do at least as well, if not better than capitalist-minded operators and generate positive results when necessary. They really wanted to show record profits for this half nationalised entity, which by a domino effect would propel this French nationalised company to the top for economic "efficiency", all the more so as all the other nationalised companies were posting abyssal losses. This would then act as a good political communication towards the international business community and "comrades" from the party and the trade unions encouraging them to deliver. Conclusion from their side: stretch the depreciation as long as possible under French accounting and tax law to above 30 years, thus minimising the charge to P&L and mechanically boosting the profit to its maximum. The Americans had a totally different view sitting on the opposite side of the board table. They were after the cash. For them the more cash the better. They just did not care about the profit that year, they had enough generated by other subsidiaries elsewhere in the world. Squeezing more cash out of the joint venture was extremely simple mechanically: the board of directors of the joint venture had only a resolution to make on the accelerating depreciation, a scheme perfectly legal in France. The entire billion-dollar investment would then be written off in just a few years. The depreciation charge would be intense in the first years, thus profit levels close to zero, and the profit tax burden to pay out to the French state would be nil or virtually nil (an ironical situation). Thus no tax payment, but much more cash, as the French corporate tax was 50% in those days. As simple as 123. Along with the joint venture chairman of the board and CEO, who was appointed every 6 months on a rotational basis (6 month a Frenchman, 6 month an American), our controller was sitting in the middle, physically and symbolically. One can easily imagine the psychological pressure, especially when presenting results of multiple economic, financial and tax simulations in this particular context. Thirty years later he remembers every detail of that day and that night (since the negotiations run until the next morning) as if it was yesterday. This was of course not the case of the other companies nationalised by the French socialo-communist government, they were all about to reveal abyssal losses. The US/French joint venture was the exception to the rule and stood as a symbol. The point is the conflict of interest between parties: those which are obvious from the beginning and those that were not planned even in the wildest nightmares and that can occur because circumstances change radically.

7.4.2 Reporting lines

Under no circumstances should the joint venture controller report hierarchically to only one of the partners as a golden rule. The worse possible case is that the joint venture controller reports hierarchically to the HQ group controller of one of the parties. If so the loyalty of the person is immediately lost, regardless of his/her quality. The moment the controller's loyalty is lost, the quality and the value of his/her input for the joint venture's interests, as an entity, is at best pointless. Even if no attempt to corrupt loyalty is made, the suspicion will always hover around the other party. This is the wisest thing to do: make the controller report solely to the joint venture CEO and make sure she/he comes originally from one of the partnering groups and that he/she will get punished/rewarded afterwards exclusively on competences when if he/she returns to the group because of insider information or "facilitating" attitude. In the preceding mini case, the controller, actually the author himself, was reporting to the joint venture chairman of the board and CEO of the joint venture, whoever this person was, since they were changing every 6 months.

7.4.3 Background

Excellent technical skills are a prerequisite in economics, management or accounting. Legal background is always a plus, if not a must. In any joint venture the founding contract (articles of incorporation) is key, as well as all other subsequent agreements with partners or directors, such as IP, supplies, management fees, shared services, etc.

An engineering background is not a must, it depends on how important it is to understand the technology of the joint venture if it is linked with engineering or design or manufacturing.

7.4.4 Cross-cultural qualities

These are key elements especially in the case of international joint ventures, where there is a permanent interface and confrontation of both corporate cultures and national cultures. This is even more so the case for the controller where joint ventures are made between partners with explicit, high context, high PDI, high individualistic cultures and the new partners who have implicit, low PDI, collectivist cultures. In some cases, by Western standards it is not even clear who the real partners are, since they may be partners only on paper, ones mentioned in the articles of incorporation; they might not be the real ultimate stakeholders. Appearances and realities might differ enormously in regions such as Russia, central Asia, south Asia, China and the Middle East for lots of excellent reasons.

Understanding more than one dimension is important, needless to say that language capabilities other than proficiency in US GAAPs or electronic spreadsheets is a real necessity.

7.5 The international project controller

7.5.1 Role

A project is a moment in the life of an organisation that has a beginning and an end. No project is made to last forever (contrary to programmes that can last indefinitely). The time span of a project can be short, lasting only minutes (a sunny afternoon at the beach) or long (decades sending man to the moon or Mars or elsewhere and return). Typically a project able to deliver its goals bases itself on an ad hoc project organisation. This project would typically cut across the regular communication lines of the organisation, and draw on multiple variables and competent resources whether adequate or required.

In summary, a project is an organisational object evanescent in contour, time and resources. It is in itself a complex constitution.

There are three basic naturally conflicting forces that the project management team (i.e., the project manager and the controller) must converge. These are:

(1) Time
(2) Resources
(3) Funding.

The project team's challenge is to create a stable core project team connected to a variable team, sometimes a loose network, and make it work harmoniously to deliver on time, on budget and with the right quality management. All this with rarely having neither the authority on people (they are "on loan" from other fixed organisations, departments, functions, etc.) nor on funding which again depends mainly on internal or external "sponsors". When the project is international in both scope and cross-border activity, the potential conflicts of interests and cultures are paramount and permanent. It is common place to know that when a project runs smoothly, nobody tends to be interested in the project core team (not even think of being grateful to them), and when it derails, the scapegoat is automatically designated: the project team and its leader! Politically minded managers tend to avoid such career pathos as international project management positions, as exposure is high and real competences and multiple skills are needed. International project management is amongst the most difficult jobs to carry out successfully. Thus the controller must demonstrate clear monitoring capabilities of those three conflicting factors: time, use of resources and use of funds. The point is of course not to merely record these three factors independently of each other but to connect them in a sensible management manner.

For example, using 70% of resources measured by competencies and allocating 70% of funds whilst spending 70% of the time planning does not mean that the project is 100% on track. If only 50% of the requested deliverables or functionalities are actually achieved, the controller lags by 30%! Whilst this already assumes it is known that 50% of the functionalities have actually been achieved. In a real situation even the progress or completion status is sometimes unknown, or at best "guestimated" by site engineers. The essential point is to know how much deliverables is produced at any one point in time over the globe. It is key for the controller to perform this role, otherwise he/she performs only spreadsheet management, does not control and even does less monitoring. Forecasting and scenario building are essential and agility and reactivity paramount. Getting information under control is not equal to crunching gigabytes of data per nanosecond, especially if international projects are developing in regions where 97% of the information is culturally of a qualitative nature and not in of a formatted quantitative data type – thus "mind the gap!"

The capacity to solve problems is also important, especially as international project will develop over a lifetime with unplanned problems. The only thing certain thing when embarking on an international project is that the controller will have to cope with uncertainty, and it should be remembered that some cultures cope more easily than others with uncertainty.

Mini case: When more means less, and less means better

A global project was being managed in an engineering company and during this period a conflict of views between the south Vietnamese- and the Swiss teams on how to solve a resource issue was experienced. The team lagged on time, but was better off on the budget. To speed up the Swiss team, a suggestion to join up with the Germans was advocated to dramatically increase the number of team members on the specific issue that had to be solved. The simple equation was that more resource equals more mandays that equates to less time used for the task, thus catch up is guaranteed. This is a classical Prussian army approach or brute force approach of "Just more of it will do the job". The Vietnamese had a chronic shortage of everything, money, technologies, equipment, etc. They had always been used to doing more with less for decades. The only thing they had in excess was courage and brainpower. Their culture was to always focus on only one point at a time – solve it, then move on to the next; this traditional attitude was inspired from years of resistance to foreign invasions where they were always outnumbered. Their proposition was completely the opposite in terms of focusing on the specific problem of the task by reducing the number of people working on the other tasks. The French, however, did not come with any immediate advise at all, preferring to involve everyone in commissions and sub-committees, to spend an enormous amount of time defining the profound notion of being on time or not on time, and then to develop a generic methodology to solve the problem of the task. This is the classical "Cartesian" approach by René Descartes. By the time they came back with a generic concept framework for a structured, supposedly universal solution that would also apply to this particular case, the case had long been resolved. Who had the right approach? In that case, the Vietnamese were correct. Their method was followed and the task was finished "bang on time".

7.5.2 So why is this the case?

Because they quickly understood that the problem in monitoring an international project is directly linked to a number of communication points – a person is a communication point. When a project team is increased by one person, the number of the communication's volume is increased by a square of the volume! Thus if "n" is the number of communication points, the number of communication lines is $\frac{1}{2}n \times (n - 1)$. If "$n$" is high, the value of the expression is then close to $\frac{1}{2}n^2$. In other words, the higher the number of people used on a project, the higher the coordination effort required.

7.5.3 Reporting lines

Identical to the joint venture case, the project controller must only report to the project director. Otherwise a conflict of interests immediately arises, putting the whole project in jeopardy.

7.5.4 Background

A great amount of business and controlling experience coupled with an excellent mental agility is essential before anything else.

MBA and/or an accountancy, engineering or lawyer's background will help.

7.5.5 Cross-cultural qualities

To possess these qualities is just paramount. Cultural interfaces are absolutely everywhere. At every corner, a cultural element will be found: in national cultures, where the project spans, national cultures of the project team's participants, organisational cultures across the project will span, as well as corporate cultures that will have to be understood and respected, etc. Diplomacy and persuasion will be the only tools used, brute force must be excluded as part of the tool box, and if borrowed or applied it will only make things worse and backfire, unless used in very specific circumstances. Seniority and great experience in having dealt in critical situations before are prerequisites.

Here gain, a good sense of humour is really necessary.

Summary

International controller's positions differ in scope according to their respective functions.

However, they all have the cross-cultural dimension in common which is paramount to carry out these functions correctly.

One of the main reasons for not being able to easily fill the aforementioned positions is that cross-cultural competencies are primarily learnt through experience today. It is possible to teach cross-cultural skills in specialised courses, but these teachings are not very often part of an accountancy, MBA or engineering study's core curriculum.

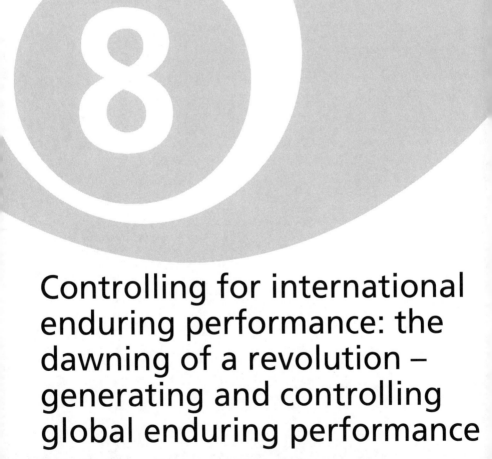

Controlling for international enduring performance: the dawning of a revolution – generating and controlling global enduring performance

Over years of international management practice either as an executive, a consultant or scholar, the author was first intrigued, then almost obsessed by a simple but not yet (fully) answered question:

Why are certain organisations, and in particular international corporations (MNCs) surviving over a century and maintaining a top performance and others not?

Of course, this question is dependent on whether life will ever exist for more than a century on the earth from now as mankind has never faced a comparable challenge as the one posed to man by himself in whole of history. This question of controlling the environment will be discussed in Chapter 9, because here controllers also have a challenge to face as well as a key role to play in guiding, monitoring and controlling corporations on the way to eco-development and eco-efficiency.

The most striking fact is that the question of enduring performance has not been completely addressed even if the remarkable work of Jim Collins and Jerry Porras (1994) is taken into consideration from thebook *Built to Last* and *From Good to Great* by Jim Collins. This study was indeed a breakthrough but it did not cover the cross-cultural factors and the international dimension as nearly all the 1400 corporations analysed and thus "selected" were North American, in particular United States with one or two exceptions. It would therefore appear that the cultural bias was there, which begs the question: Was the US model for excellence universal? Knowing that most of the "selected" iconic corporations had an overwhelming home/United States cultural imprint, and that the bulk of their business was made domestically in the United States with relatively little cross-border span, it can be safely assumed that this is not the case.

It is a fact that the root cause or causes for such an enduring performance could not arise from a technological edge only, because over a century any technology, regardless of how advanced and protected (IP), ends up becoming common and public knowledge.

It is also a fact that an unbroken track record of superior performance over more than a century could not be attributable to the charisma and inspiration of a single leader, as the time span far exceeds human life expectancy.

It therefore had to come from something else: a special or series of factors. Not "hard factors" which rust over time, but rather from "soft factors" which give a long-lasting imprint. It was decided to investigate the cultures and values route (and particularly the intersect/interface of corporate cultures and national cultures).

This chapter discusses how 12 fundamental culturally connected factors explain to maintain an enduring top-level international performance. This is an outcome of an extensive project spanning over 4 years and cutting across cultures, continents and centuries in those companies' performances; and performance drivers have been analysed over a time frame of 100–150 years.

The valuable findings are that these 12 factors rank along dimensions and can be qualified and quantified individually, giving birth to the N12 MODEL.

For every single international company, a diagnostic score can now be established to show if this given company is likely or not to be successful on a long-term basis.

One can easily see that multiple applications are possible.

A naturally obvious application is the M&A field; however, as seen in Chapter 7, above 75% of M&As fail to deliver the expected results, mostly due to cultural mismanagement.

The N12 MODEL gives all types of managers, controllers and analysts, who are operating in a multinational cross-cultural context, a powerful conceptual model and a practical tool to be in control of performance of the real key factors: those which drive enduring performance and that are conducive to, inter alia, deliver, year after year, top class cash flows, P&Ls and balance sheets as well as quality, personnel, client and other stakeholders satisfaction.

The process, the conceptual model as well as the analysis and prognosis tools is discussed step by step in the following sections.

But firstly a question has to be asked: What really is an international business-enduring performance?

8.1 What really is an international business-enduring performance?

This question may sound odd and even trivial but the answer is, however, not that straightforward.

In the current environment, everyone talks of performance, even in areas where performance has no particular place such as health, education, religion, etc.

Performance today, in terms of business and management in western societies, is exclusively associated with financial performance, i.e., the share value. If the value of the company shares goes up at the stock exchange, the company is said to be performing. This concept of performance cascades down to all managers and employees in the civil society as well as in the individual's private life.

This exclusively financial view of performance is in fact fairly recent.

Today, Corporate America is literally owned by "institutional investors". John C. Bogle (2005), founder and chairman of Vanguard Group, in his address to the 20th Anniversary meeting of the Council of Institutional Investors on April 11th in Washington, DC, says that funds were holding 66% of US stocks in 2005.

In 1932, based on the remarkable landmark study of Berie and Means – the modern corporation and private property – there no was share held by an institutional investor.

In 1960, institutional investors held 8% of America's corporate shares.
In 1985, institutional investors held 24%.
In 2005, institutional investors held 66%.

Out of the trillions of dollars that change hands in the world everyday, 97% of them are not linked to any real underlying business transaction. These money exchanges are directed towards the sole financial transactions themselves instead. This shift is fairly recent and resembles a tidal wave which fundamentally rocks the whole society's values and structures: financial performance tends to be synonymous to performance. However, corporate performance is multifaceted. Depending on time phases and cultural areas, performance can be based on the following.

8.1.1 Social

This was in Henry Ford's case, where a lot of attention was given to the fact that his employees were well paid (above average), even if one desired side effect was wished it would be that they could buy a T Ford car with the surplus cash on their pay slips. This was also the concept adopted in France at the beginning of the industrial era where large industrial, privately owned companies used to provide housing, education, recreation, medical care and private pension to their employees and their families. (Such was the case with Michelin and Corons du Nord.) They actually created the "social security" long before the state. In Japan, it is still understood that employment is a mutual lifelong commitment. Large Japanese conglomerates are interlinked with other key society structures such as universities, research institutes, social engineering organisations, schooling, housing, medical care, pensions, insurances and banks. Performance is primarily and definitely social in line with their "collectivist" culture as defined by the Hofstede's model. In Sweden, a low PDI, with high "collectivist" and "feminine/farmer" indices (as per the Hofstede classification) performance is part of a social role to society. They pioneered the "work enrichment" concept where teams of co-workers would autonomously assemble a complete engine, gear box or vehicle, e.g., in the automotive industry (Volvo).

8.1.2 Industrial and technical

Industrial performance has always been a source of pride and a competitive advantage. The automaker Citroën organised the "Croisière Noire", in 1928, and the "Croisière Jaune", in 1931, which were a series of rally-raids that crossed the whole of Africa and Asia (over 30 000 km each) to demonstrate Citroën's superiority in its vehicle's transmission systems and for having in those days the most advanced vehicle in the world. The same applies today to Formula 1 racing or round the globe sailing races, etc. The increasing influence of corporate sponsoring has even reinforced this facet of the industrial performance to promote it further and build bigger images, often far from reality. Who can reasonably connect a Renault's multiple Formula 1 hard won racing champion titles on speed tracks to the 60 hp diesel powering a Renault van on Paris's day-by-day overcongested ring road (called périphérique) crawling at 5 mph, at best!

8.1.3 Quality

Quality performance can be seen as an incarnation of technological or industrial performance. The concept of quality dates back to the dawn of mankind. The best quality tool (e.g., an unbreakable sword made of the best quality steel) would have competitive advantage to survival or domination. Modern day's quality concept was revived by Deming, an American scholar who brought the quality thinking to post-World War II Japan, as part of the Mac Arthur team. Starting from Japan where the brute statistical elements of Deming (1986) in a Kaizen holistic philosophy were incorporated, the concept of quality started conquering the world in the 1980s and has become a major element in business strategy and operations.

8.1.4 Perceived performance

Image perception and image building is paramount. This has become one of the key drivers of the 20th and 21st centuries. It is entering into the lives of all and has many incarnations from the use of movie stars to help sell instant coffee, cosmetics, UN programs or win elections, to the brute advertising force and management by opinion and mind controlling.

An image perception index of businesses does exist, and is updated every year by the economic sector. This is the highly respected and coveted "most admired company" ranking orchestrated by a prominent US press group.

8.1.5 Economic performance

This is the concept everyone is familiar with today. However, economic performance is different from financial performance. Economic performance is best illustrated in the long run by the EBIT (Earnings Before Interests and Taxes) or the EBITDA (Earnings Before Interests Taxes, Depreciation and Amortisation). EBIT and EBITDA give a robust indication on a firm's ability to perform economically and intrinsically without introducing external variables such as financing and ownership. EBIT and EBITDA are the fundamentals that are used to value companies by the "multiples" method. EBITDA is also a reliable precursor of the business's cash flow, as working capital variations do smooth out and can be considered neutral in the long run. An early cash flow marker, EBITDA is also the building brick to company and business valuation, using this time DCF (discounted cash flows) methods since cash flows and EBITDA have a common DNA. An alternative to the EBIT/EBITDA is the relative EBIT/EBITDA (or any other form of economic performance marker) compared to the investment, characterised by the famous ROI (return on investment). Whilst working at an American MNC called Du Pont de Nemours, in 1919, engineer Donaldson Brown was the initiator of ROI as a performance indicator, control and monitoring tool. It was a breakthrough at the time and it was the first time ever that a company made economic performance monitoring part of industrial and management issues. Secondly, it was the first time ever that a company invested in management science as part of corporate R&D, and more specifically in the controlling science field. Although conceptually not balanced to perfection, ROI is a very convenient tool (ROI relates to instant positioning in terms of the assets on the balance sheet and a flow of profit in a given period) because mechanically and practically, it puts EBIT and its main contributors in relationship. Furthermore it allows to segment the efforts and contributions of all employees and to cascade the performance targets throughout the organisation. ROCE (return on capital employed) is a more recent incarnation of ROI that generally bases itself on the same concept but brings only few refinements.

8.1.6 Financial performance

This is completely different. It was initially thought that financial performance was related to the financial investment and its return, regardless of its economic or industrial application. This was classically the case when companies would float capital at the stock exchange and promise financial returns (in the form of dividends or capital gains) in exchange for capital investment and where past performance would be the best precursor of future performance and thus a quasi-guarantee to raise capital in good conditions when needed. This gave rise to the PER (price to earning ratio) as a performance indicator.

Enduring international corporate performance relates to corporations which have managed to maintain the highest standard of performance in all these fields, decade after decade and sometimes for over more than a century.

8.2 The fundamental underlying drivers behind the "everlasting" success: the N12 MODEL

To investigate about the core drivers of this long-term enduring performance, factors which were either technologically dependent or connected to a specific charismatic leader were not concentrated on, it was instead on those which were more profound. The international span of the business was focussed on to ensure that no confusion took place in terms of the root cause – those 12 factors – and the effects: the EBIT sequences, the ROIs, the share value compared to the industry average, the perceived performance, etc.

Twelve canonical factors emerged after more than 4 years of research in multi-industrial sectors and using multi-criteria data and information analyses, including scanning through 150 years of annual accounts as well as analysing thousands of archive folios and communications, interviewing board members and top executives of leading international MNCs, discussing with top academics in European, American, Asia and Pacific business schools.

They belong to three main sectors which explain the root cause for enduring international performance (Figure 8.1).

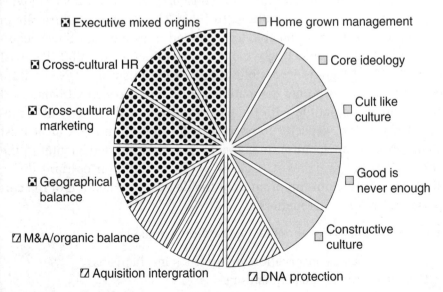

Figure 8.1 N12 MODEL.

Sector A: Corporate culture and values

Comprises five factors or dimensions which relate to corporate culture and values, of which four had already been identified in substance by Jim Collins, i.e.:

(1) Home-grown management
(2) Core ideology
(3) Cult-like cultures
(4) Good is never enough
(5) And constructive culture having already been identified by Prof. Cooke.

Sector B: Corporate DNA Conservation

This sector covers those factors that are essential for a corporation to persist. They can take many forms, ranging from mechanism to obstruct or limit the possibility of "foreigners" taking control over the share capital; e.g., privately owned companies such as the Mars/Master food corporation, votes limited to national shareholders, multiple voting rights versus no voting right shares, circular shareholding (keiretsu), special links with the state (nationalisation, monopoly), IP via countless international licensees and trademarks, size (a corporation the size of Nestlé can hardly be bought without prior consent). This sector also includes aspects of acquisition integration. To avoid 75% or above failure rate in M&As, it is essential to be able to target and integrate only those acquisitions that can be effectively metabolised. Different possibilities exist to make this integration possible: small-size acquisitions, DNA/culture of national and corporate compatible acquisitions, pace and balance of acquisitions compatible with the pace and the actual capacity of corporate assimilation, capacity to encode in the corporate DNA or at least some DNA of the acquired target as long as it is not detrimental to the corporation but enriches it (e.g., to gain leveraging on cultural diversity). The form is not important, but the degree of protection of the corporation DNA is what matters.

This sector comprises three factors or dimensions, i.e.:

Corporate DNA conservation and defence mechanisms
Capacity to integrate acquisitions
Acquisitions versus organic growth balance.

Sector C: International and cross-cultural interfaces

By definition this sector is also essential for companies whose business cuts across cultures in different countries and continents. The adequate management of cultural intersects and interfaces is important, and comprises four elements, i.e.:

(1) Geographical spread balance
(2) Integrative cross-cultural marketing mix
(3) Human resources cross-cultural management
(4) Culturally diverse executive board.

We will now look at the scope and definition of each of these 12 dimensions in more detail, which is sectioned out into three main sectors:

8.2.1   Sector A: Corporate culture and values

Home-grown management

Definition
This relates to the corporation's ability to fill up the upper echelons of the command chain (CEO and executive board) with high calibre managers that have made their way up through the ranks of the organisation during their entire employment life AND ensuring that they have been exposed to different roles, functions and countries.

Toyota is a case in point where ALL the highest ranking officers started directly with Toyota after leaving college and have worked their way up the corporate ladder. It is the same with Scania, Nestlé and Kraft.

Core ideology

Definition
Core ideology is the existence of a very strong set of beliefs, values and ideas which transcend and drive the business components and the organisation over time and geographical boundaries, regardless of specific circumstances. This set of values, beliefs and ideas exudes throughout the whole organisation, crossing all sections, functions and echelons.

Example: Kaizen is the core ideology for Toyota which has driven the corporation to enduring and outstanding success across boundaries and time.

Cult like cultures

Definition

Some corporate cultures are deep-rooted and used as if they were "cults".

Here we are particularly interested to focus on the WAY in which an ideology is used by looking at three main components:

- A pantheon: through using a set of gods/deities in all available circumstances by which the corporation and its components are abiding. In the case of companies this would be market share, share price, PER, share holder value, EVA, quality, market share and client satisfaction. These would be emphasised through incarnating current or past heroes/champions or by cultivating stories of past heroic figures (mythology).
- A creed: through the existence of a "mission" statement, e.g., whereby setting the official "faith" or doctrine.
- A structure: thorough communication to spread the ideology (corporate manuals, internal magazines, on line CEO speeches), a clergy (a cast of employees who are vectors who uphold and spread the ideology, train the laymen, help the employees to deepen their knowledge and practice of the "path/faith", e.g., the "black belts" and the "masters black belts" in the Six Sigma methodology), a set of rituals (the budget process, the annual conventions, the inner grades and levels, successive promotions and initiations, corporate dress code: the grey suits) and "temples" such as corporate or internal universities/academies, induction seminars, etc.

Note that the structure is different from the preceding one of the creed and pantheon which spread the core ideology, where the latter is now focusing on the apparatus and structures meant and devised to (relatively) efficiently deploy and anchor the corporate culture stemming out of the core ideology.

At Toyota the TPS is a cult-like element (Toyota Production System, recently renamed The Toyota way) whereas Kaizen is the core ideology.

Good is never enough

Definition

This factor is characteristic of management and the employees' attitudes who are always looking towards improvements, although the current situation could be considered as satisfactory or comfortable. These improvements can be of a financial, economic, technological, marketing, quality, social or environmental nature. Here we are not focused on the result but the attitude vis à vis improvement. Toyota Kaizen (meaning constant improvement) is once again a perfect example of this attitude.

Constructive culture

Definition

Here we refer to the work of Professor R. Cooke, from Chicago, who proved that a "constructive" culture contributed to long-term superior performance.

A "constructive" culture is characterised by the following subsets:

- *Achievement*: Employees are expected to set challenging but realistic goals and establish plans to reach those goals as well as pursue them with enthusiasm.
- *Self-actualising*: Employees are expected to enjoy their work, develop themselves and take on new interesting tasks.
- *Humanistic-encouraging*: Employees are expected to be supportive, constructive and open to influence their dealings with one another.
- *Affiliating*: Employees are expected to be friendly, cooperative and sensitive to the satisfaction of their work group.

8.2.2 Sector B: Corporate DNA conservation

"Corporate DNA" conservation and defence mechanisms

This factor specifically relates to an organisation's capacity to preserve its "corporate genetic imprint" against external offences. Although it is difficult to qualify exactly what a corporate DNA or genetic print may be, it is however clear that corporations tend to protect their identity and independence in the form of constant struggle for survival (survival of the fittest like attitude).

Conservation and defence mechanisms were achieved through three major methods:

(1) Setting up juridical (e.g., selective voting rights) or financial (e.g. cross capital stakes, closed capital) or political (e.g., lobbies, state control, public opinion) efficient gimmicks that are protective measures to prevent the corporation from being taken over or from a hostile raid, or from being acquired, and thus avoid the board of directors being swept out.
(2) Setting up highly protective measures/policies regarding IP.
(3) Setting up high entry barriers (e.g., norms, monopoly, lobby).

Capacity to integrate acquisitions

Definition

For those corporations whose acquisitions or mergers represent a substantial part of their development mode, this factor focuses on the capacity to successfully integrate newly acquired business.

For example, Nestlé is a corporation that has made substantial acquisitions over the years, all of which have always been integrated seamlessly. In this field, Nestlé is probably the best in the world, whereas the DaimlerChrysler merger has seen enormous difficulties.

Acquisitions versus balance of organic growth

This factor tends to assess the balance of growth over a long period of time (50 years or more) between organic growth and growth through acquisitions.

For example, Toyota has an exclusively organic growth model, whereas Volkswagen has grown substantially through acquisitions (SEAT, SKODA, AUDI, BENTLEY, etc.) and has had fluctuating success.

8.2.3   Sector C: International and cross-cultural interface

Geographical balance/spread of the business

Definition

This factor concentrates on assessing that even if an international corporation operates and sells in a number of foreign countries (e.g., over a hundred), it makes the vast majority of its revenues and cash flow in its country of origin; although the corporation achieves its international business in a quasi-evenly spread manner over the globe.

Example: Wal-Mart, the number one in worldwide retail distribution is operating internationally on a sporadic basis although vastly concentrating within its origin market, the United States. However, the French retail distributor Carrefour is also operating globally, but France is a minority share of its turnover and cash flow.

Integrative cross-cultural marketing

Definition
A corporation operating and marketing internationally has to successfully integrate different national/ethnic cultural factors into its marketing mix.

Localising the marketing mix to local ethnic cultural traits or geographical structures might be assessed through the balance of local versus global items in the products/services portfolio/offering. The same as to selling/advertising/promotion/distribution/pricing attributes.

Example: McDonald's restaurants localise at least 50% of their offering to adapt to local tastes, conditions and cultures (alcoholic beverage are served in certain countries, Apenzel Swiss cheese–based cheeseburgers are sold only in Switzerland, burgers without beef in India, etc.) as well as pricing, a key element in McDonald's marketing mix, is tailored to local net disposable income expressed as a fraction of the hourly base wage (the famous Mc Do index).

This is the same with the automotive industry, e.g., the Gol Volkswagen is specific to Brazil.

Human resource cross-cultural management

Definition
This factor deals with the capacity an internationally selling and operating corporation has in assigning managerial positions outside their country of origin as well as establishing this as a structured policy. To an extent, it may be considered that cross-border and cross-cultural

transfers offer the possibility to climb the organisation's ladder and achieve higher management levels.

For example, Royal Dutch Shell has a long-term established policy of cross-cultural/cross-border transfer policies for managers.

Culturally diverse executive board

Definition

This factor is basically very different from the preceding one, because here it takes into consideration the capacity that an internationally operating and marketing corporation at its highest management level has to elaborate and pursue balanced (thus efficient in terms of long-standing performance) strategies, views, policies and executive styles through a truly culturally diverse executive board, reflected by the different cultures of its members.

For example, this is the case for a global luxury goods leader, such as the Richemont group, where the executive board is made of culturally diverse members.

8.3 The new control keys "soft" factors last longer than "hard" factors, scoring the N12 MODEL, the I^2Q, diagnostic, prognostic and remedies

Now that the 12 canonical factors (dimensions) that determine and qualify the long-term performance of an international corporation have been established, it is time to evaluate the intensity with which an MNC is engaged on each on these areas.

Given the nature of each dimension, it is not practical to use a linear measure for each axis. However, it is perfectly possible to use a scale that is commonly employed in the social science intensity scaling – the "Likert" scaling system (Likert, 1961). Briefly, the "Likert" scaling system gives a *relative* scaling. For example, a factor can be either measured as very low, low, medium low, medium, medium high or high, etc., giving up to 10 *relative* positions.

This method is very commonly used, e.g., in opinion polls to evaluate product impact vis à vis customers and end users, or in political science to evaluate the favourable/unfavourable balance of opinions regarding a political leader. A similar kind of relative scale is also used in medical emergencies, where the patient is asked to self-evaluate the intensity of the pain on a 1–10 scale before calling the doctor on duty in relation to the evaluated pain. Given the nature of the data the same approach is used in this case.

In the N12 MODEL, each of the 12 individual dimensions is scaled with a ranking from 1 to 10.

The maximum standard composite score is therefore 120.

The I^2Q, *I*nternational *I*ntercultural *Q*uotient, is the final quotient of the corporation's actual score (e.g., 90) on the maximum possible score (in that case 120), equating in that particular case to 75% (cf example A versus B). This very simple example assumes that each of the 12 dimensions is of equal importance (weight).

But more generally, it is useful to adjust the relative weight of each dimensional factor to reflect specific businesses or economic sector conditions. The 12 axes identified on the N12 MODEL graph drive a company's international long-haul performance and are robust, which means that they do not depend on the company's activity. However, their relative importance may differ from one field of activity to another. For instance, it is obvious that the international marketing integrative dimension depending on people's cultural expectations is much more important for a company in the food or cosmetics industry than for a company selling electronic chips that end up inside a computer.

A linear combination of the weighted scores gives a measure of the company's international performance.

$$I^2Q = \sum_{i=1}^{12} \alpha_i x_i$$

where α_1 is the weight of the axis i and x_1 the score of the company on this axis; where of course $\sum_{i=1}^{12} = 100\%$.

This allows expressing the I^2Q as a mark out of 10, which then multiplied by 10 makes it easy to read and employ as performance percentage (quotient).

The advantage of this is that it allows instant inter-businesses and cross-industry comparisons and informed benchmarks.

Several other measures can then be computed from the data to highlight a company's complete international profile. The purpose of this book is not to go into too much detail, but to show the general approach. More details or precisions on the N12 MODEL methodology can be obtained at the EC^2M Institute or directly from the author.

8.3.1   Interpretation

The first level of analysis and interpretation is the overall composite score stated by the I^2Q which needs to be above 50% to allow a promising perspective. However, a minimum critical score must be achieved in each dimension (e.g., critical factor depending on industrial sector), otherwise a score too low on a single dimension would jeopardise the entire model since the overall coherence would then not be achieved although the total comprehensive I^2Q may be satisfactory.

The second level of interpretation of the model is of course on a dimension per dimension basis.

The score achieved is only an indication as the profound understanding on each dimension needs to be done with a sense of judgment. But it gives very precious indications on, firstly, where the company stands today, in which direction progresses should be made and with what level of intensity.

The N12 MODEL is a tool for controllers and their management to assess, diagnose, benchmark, prognose, control and monitor performance on their international corporation which is on the way to enduring success, by addressing the root causes and canonical drivers in a structured way.

A conceptual model and its applicative tool such as the N12 MODEL and the associated scoring system I^2Q was not available until today. The only tools that were made available to controllers in the majority of cases were only cost and financial models that address the outcome actions in an exclusively financial and economic way (with the exception of balanced score cards discussed in Chapter 2), and they are only short-term oriented (quarterly driven corporations). The current situation's assessment is already of a great help because it allows the corporation management to have an unbiased picture of where their company stands at any moment. It is also very useful to run the N12 MODEL and I²Q across the organisation by sampling different hierarchical levels, different functions, different geographies, etc. This exercise has proven very interesting as it often reveals profound disparities between all these different segments and layers of the organisation in many cases. Such disparities are of course by themselves a cause for under-sustained performance because the fundamental dimensions are not in synchronisation.

Running N12 MODEL and I²Q at only the executive board of the international HQ is therefore not enough, and can even be misleading, because the whole corporation, to be efficient, must work together along the same lines.

Of the 12 factors that drive the enduring international performance, most of them are culturally related and are known as the "soft factors". Very seldom are "hard" factors, such as IRR (internal rate of return), technology, cycle times, IP and the like used.

This is food for thought, as the basic role of a controller should be to control and monitor the relevant factors, those factors that drive the performance and secure the future. ...

A revolution is dawning and there is an exciting perspective ahead for controllers interested in facing the challenges of the 21st century.

8.4 How to implement the new grid: monitor your cultural factors

Scaling the relative intensity along each of the 12 dimensions is not a straightforward task, as this is a new perspective; neither a ready-made nor pre-formatted standard.

Experience shows that the scaling process requires investing time and effort and that it is a heuristic process. Some of the dimensions are easier to scale than others. It may be easier in a company to give a measure of the executive board of its culturally diverse origin, taking into account easily quantifiable sub-elements such as the number of expatriated years of each executive board member, their nationality, their years of exposure to international projects, the number of languages spoken, etc.; or the aspects of integrative cross-cultural marketing through measuring the number of products that are localised according to the "home" corporate portfolio, etc. Showing assessment of DNA protection on the scale grid may require less experience as it comprises easily quantifiable elements, e.g., relative to IP (number of licenses, patents, trademarks, proprietary technologies) with other key elements of a more qualitative nature (circular capital stakes, voting exclusions, etc.).

Implementing this new control grid is a project in itself that requires a planned structured approach. Each company is different, but ultimately the end result is the same. Once the grid and the initial scaling have been established, it is very powerful to benchmark units or segments within a corporation.

In the event that one or more of the several dimensions are below the 50% threshold, an interesting phase commences for the controller in conjunction with his colleagues; as to identifying the action levers to bridge the performance gap dimension per dimension, and to devise action plans to address the root causes over a time frame more like a planning and budgeting exercise – except that the scope is more profound and the tools and measurement metrics are not the classical P&Ls, balance sheets and cash flow statements. It is a cross-functional exercise by nature where line management as well as human resource management are involved.

Mini case: The Global Food champion is a 150-years-old giant. Its closest contender on the global scene has just turned 200 years old ...

When analysing the different world players in the food business, an excellent example of applying the N12 MODEL can be found.

Interestingly enough, fairly recent firms and MNCs have been founded only 150 or even 200 years ago in the food business.

In our example, the worldwide leading firm "A" is a Giant MNC founded 150 years ago, originating in Europe. By all standards and over an extraordinarily long period, even under different CEOs, "A" has dominated the global sector, . The second MNC, firm "B", comes from the United States. It is also a giant operating (less) globally, and has a very good performance. It constantly performs better than the market and has been in existence for almost 200 years.

However "A" dwarfs "B" in all aspects of performance: market share, market development, EBIT, return on sales, ROCE, P/E, share price evolution, quality, innovation, etc.

"A" also has a geographical spread with its balance quasi-perfectly and evenly distributed all over the world, whereas "B" although an MNC, is still doing 75% of its business domestically in the United States. Almost all "A's" product lines are localised in composition, packaging, distribution, tastes, colours, communication, prices, etc. – note that the food business has a strong interface with local cultures since food is a highly social element as a social pillar and integrator. "'B's" product range has only a 12% localisation resulting in a strong American "taste", which reflects on advertising, packaging, communication and flavours.

Both "A" and "B" have grown organically and via acquisitions. However, "A's" acquisitions have been targeted and integrated perfectly in a seamless way, enriching "A's" core DNA, without diluting its core corporate culture. "A" is a quasi-perfect illustration of leveraging on cultures.

"B" regularly fears that it could disappear either by a merger of "equals" with competitors "C" or "D", or become controlled by a fund, or even become consolidated by a fund with competitors "E" or "F". In contrast, "A" has managed a remarkably multi-tiered DNA preservation system through IP and most importantly by circular financial stakes with another stable global MNC leader, in another consumer market (cosmetics). It also has a very stringent system restricting voting rights to a very small circle of shareholders, taking full advantage of the almost tailored state-level legal provisions. As a final measure, the hyper size of "A" makes it quasi-impossible to be absorbed by another corporation.

> Thus, despite the fact that "B" is a superb company in its own right, it is no match with "A".
>
> This is no wonder:
>
> - "A" has an I^2Q of 95%, whereas "B" has an I^2Q of 54%.
> - By going further into the N12 MODEL analysis it is interesting to note that "B" lags seriously in many key factors.
> - Until these are addressed and remedied or improved "B" will always lag behind "A" (Figure 8.2).

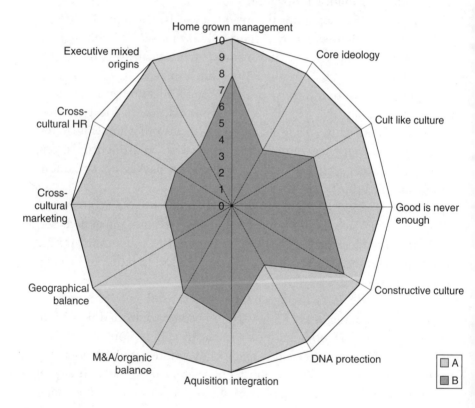

Figure 8.2 A versus B I^2Q.

Another obvious application is in applying the N12 MODEL before the deal to dramatically increase the success rate of international M&As as a part of their due diligences, for both the acquiring and targeted company, is made. It is only in this ex ante application that billions of dollars can be gained or saved, as the potential compatibility (or not) will appear as well as its root cause.

However, if using the N12 MODEL ex ante is not possible or not performed for any reason, it is still possible to use it ex post, i.e., after the deal has been made and the companies have merged.

Although this is less optimal because it comes after the merger, it is still possible to identify the gaps (or overlaps) of each individual dimension by mapping both N12 and I^2Q models (those of the acquirer and of the acquired) and to immediately build ad hoc programmes to address the lack in the dimension whilst remembering that time is important in M&A integration.

Summary

Top long-lasting performance for international companies is not a matter of luck or coincidence. Some MNCs succeed, whereas others do not. They either disappear or get absorbed over time. Maintaining top performance and remaining amongst the best for a maximum length of time that far exceeds the technological advantage or the drive of a once charismatic leader is a far-reaching goal. It takes a lot of work to address the real performance drivers and not just their elusive image.

Controllers and managers now have a conceptual model and an application tool – the N12 MODEL and the I^2Q – made available to them to help them perform this exciting duty in addressing, assessing, controlling, benchmarking and monitoring the *relevant* factors.

References

Bogle, J. (2005), *The Battle for the Soul of Capitalism.*
Collins, J. and Porras, J. (1994), *Built to Last.*
Deming, E. (1986), *Out of the Crisis.*
Likert, R. (1961), *New Patterns of Management.*

Controlling for the environment

Chapter 8 focused on engineering, controlling and monitoring of enduring performance of multinational corporations (MNCs), and identified the key drivers that aimed at generating a top performance over decades and centuries. It was also seen how to quantify the 12 key elements and how to monitor them as part of the controlling role. It was also learned how to quantify and measure the situation of an MNC and how to make a prognosis, as well as how to dramatically increase chances not only for long-term survival but also to achieve top performance. But it is also clear that a corporation's long-term performance cannot be seen in isolation. It has to be seen in context of a larger picture which includes the long-term performance of the global environment. How to quantify and measure the situation of an MNC vis à vis enduring top performance, and how to pose a prognosis, as well as how to dramatically increase its chances for not only long-term survival, but also top performance has been discussed. However, it would be meaningless to strive on keeping an international corporation performance at its best for over a century or more if the "planet" were to cease to exist in 20 or 30 years from now.

This is a very far-reaching subject and at first sight one could think that controlling has nothing to do with it.

The crux of the matter is that the opposite is true. As we stand at the dawn of the 21st century, scientific evidence (denied for the last 30 years but now too obvious to be any longer denied by the economic, financial, business and political communities/lobbies) is conclusive (UN/IPCC November 2007, WHO November 2007, OECD, EU, etc.) of the fact that human activities are detrimental to life. Be it global warming, the reduction in biodiversity, deforestation and desertification, pollution of seas and rivers, depletion of freshwater resources, air pollution, chemical pollution and electromagnetic pollution.

This also links with the former chapter as cultural diversity goes hand in hand with biodiversity like UNESCO stated it in its *Universal Declaration on Cultural Diversity*: "cultural diversity is as necessary for humankind as biodiversity is for nature" (UNESCO, 2001).

To be more precise the root cause pointed out by scientists is that not all is due to human activities per se. The wording has been softened to make it politically correct. Actually human activities have been taking place since the existence of mankind, which by definition, i.e., for about 140 000 years, and no drama has occurred since. The disruption in trends and the race towards a disaster has started with human *industrial* activities at the end of 19th century, with an ever-accelerating pace post-World War II.

Something has simply gone *out of control*.

The lack of control here is to be taken literally and seriously at the macro level, but not just at the economic micro level but also at the corporate level. The business community has played and is still playing a detrimental role on the environment in that it developed industrial activities per se with little or no consideration for the environment, and promoted behavioural patterns from individuals which reinforces and accelerates the stress on environment. This is especially the case within the automotive industry, tourism industry, programmed consumer electronic product obsolescence and artificially shortened life cycles, etc.

9.1 Sustainable growth: just an oxymoron?

9.1.1 Controlling for sustainability

Firstly, what is sustainable growth? The most commonly accepted and politically correct definition is known as the Brundtland Report (*Our Common Future*) which states that sustainable development is development that "meets the needs of the present without compromising the ability of future generations to meet their own needs". The Brundtland Report, named after the Chair of the World Commission on Environment and Development, was welcomed by the UN General Assembly resolution 38/161 on 19 December 1983 (UN, 1983).

Secondly, this very definition is also criticised as being an oxymoron (a self-contradicting sentence) as many argue that it is physically impossible to grow "ad infinitum".

9.2 Entropy versus infinity: Malthus, Georgescu, Meadows versus Brundtland

There is a real point here. Is endless growth physically and economically possible? Although this is the UN and governments' present creed, many scientists do not share this view. They argue that in any finite system (and the planet Earth is a finite system) infinite growth is impossible, basing their theory on thermodynamics where entropy makes it impossible. Nicholas Georgescu-Roentgen, PhD in statistics from the Sorbonne University and professor at the Van der Bilt University in the United States and at the Universities of Bucharest in Romania and Strasbourg in France, formulated the theory in connection with the laws of physics, saying that only a constant regression in growth to an equilibrium point would save the planet. He expressed this theory in the book, *The Entropy Law and the Economic Process*, published in 1971 (Georgescu-Roentgen, 1971).

Nicholas Georgescu-Roentgen was not the first to clearly formulate this profound intrinsic contradiction to Brundtland. Well before him at the dawn of modern-day economics, a Cambridge graduate scholar in mathematics, Thomas Malthus wrote in his seminal book, *An Essay on the Principle of Population* first published in 1798 (Malthus, 1798), the evidence of a mismatch between the resource (food) demand and supply function. Malthus highlighted that the growth of population was outpacing, by many times, the growth in resource (food) supply, making everlasting expansion unsustainable. The outcome according to Malthus was a future destruction of mankind. This was also predicted by Karl Marx (Marx, 1867) who stated that capitalism known as "liberalism" today, even when left alone, can only but eventually destroy itself and the whole society. Pro memoria, although coming from totally different political spectrums, Malthus and Karl Marx agreed on a common outcome in this case.

Malthus' supply and demand model influenced many prominent economists such as David Ricardo, Alfred Marshall, John Maynard Keynes, to name a few, as well as the famous scientist Charles Darwin's concept of survival of the fittest, where species competed for scarce resources, as described in his book *The Origins of the Species* (Darwin, 1859).

Closer to date, a group of MIT scientists, commissioned by the Club of Rome and headed by the Meadows, produced a breakthrough analysis in 1972 based on system dynamics and computer modelling under *Limits to Growth* (Meadows et al., 1972). At the time this highly sophisticated model showed clear evidence of the conflict resulting from rapid expansion, and its consequences, which included the problems of pollution and resource depletion, in a finite resource environment. They concluded that infinite growth was not sustainable, and that the sooner realignment to a growth was made in synchronisation with natural growth the better.

At about the same time in 1970, British scientist James Lovelock, a Fellow of the Royal Academy and employed by the NASA came up with the *Gaia Theory* (Lovelock, 1970). (Gaia is the Greek mythology name given to planet Earth, which itself comes from the even more ancient Egyptian mythology word Geb who was the goddess that created Earth.) Here Lovelock also defended a similar thesis. Lovelock more recently in 2006 advocated in his writings, *The Revenge of Gaia* (Lovelock, 2006), that it was already too late for sustainable development and that the only way to avoid a global collapse was sustainable retreat.

Today there is enough undisputable scientific evidence as never before in history, that mankind as a species and other life forms are threatened because of the industrial activities.

In 2007, the former US Vice President Al Gore with the IPCC (Intergovernmental Panel on Climate Change) was awarded the Nobel Peace Prize for his contribution to the environment; by means of a film *An Inconvenient Truth*, Al Gore crystallises the damages to the environment caused by man's industrial activities (Gore, 2006). More strikingly is the speed of global destruction that is happening under our very eyes, so visible, yet so ignored by some governments, business economists, scholars, executives and investment bankers alike.

In the same vein, another Economics Nobel Prize winner, Joseph Stiglitz, also warned about the destruction caused by globalisation in economies and societies in his seminal book, *Globalisation and Its Discontents in 2002* (Stiglitz, 2002).

This was again echoing another Economics Nobel Prize winner, Maurice Allais, in his 1999 book, *La mondialisation, la destruction des emplois et de la croissance* (globalisation, destruction of employment and growth) (Allais, 1999).

And last but not the least, the other very famous Economics Nobel Prize winner and Harvard professor, Amartya Sen (1999), who advocated for a balanced economic, social and environmental model all his life.

9.3 Nicholas Stern on environment economics: the economic argument

The distinguished British economist Sir Nicholas Stern, chartered by UK's Prime Minister Tony Blair, delivered a very comprehensive report on the economic impact and its damages on the environment in November 2006. The resulting Stern report, based on the best possible models, state-of-the-art scenarios and dynamic simulation systems available is a compelling sum of science that would take too long to go into detail in this book. However, if there was only one lesson for industry and the business community to remember that came out of the report, it would be this: The environmental situation will continue degrading but not exclusively due to global warming and climatic change, which is itself linked to our carbonised way of life (originally a Western plague, but now fast growing in emerging economies such as India and China). Decoupling is a route to pursue. This is through disconnecting the economic growth rate from the energy and carbon intensity per unit of gross domestic product (GDP) produced. However so far, de facto, all the Kyoto Protocol measures (which the United States being the world's major carbon emitter has not ratified) have failed to deliver, and especially so when considering what is currently happening in booming giant economies like China and India, which are relying massively on fossil oil to pursue their growth. As everyone knows, fossil fuels and especially coal-fired power plants are major emitters of carbon, accelerating the green house effect. China is building and starting a new carbon coal-fired power plant every month. The sooner the carbon balance is monitored and controlled, with a radical move towards a decarbonised economy, the better. Stern calculated that a 1% investment of global GDP today in environment-related issues would avoid a 20% GDP loss in the future. If this would be the case, a rate of return on the investment in environment for mankind would be 20-fold. Stern also predicted that a decrease in GDP as sharp as 20% would cause major social disruptions compared to those generated by world wars or the 1929 depression. This was echoed in December 2007 by the UN Secretary General Ban Ki Moon in his address to the UN Bali conference on climate, where he predicted a possible international civil war looming ahead, if nothing substantial was done. Stern's central economic argument is that the environmental costs are so far not taken into account in the economic equation leading to business and economic decisions. Environmental costs are considered today as "externalities". More specifically, the cost on the environment normally appears after a long lag time (sometimes decades) in relation to an initial investment. These costs should be discounted and factored back into any investment payback or return calculation.

9.4   The IIRR

An alternative eco-performance index that combines both the economic and ecological efficiency has been developed in liaison with the Global Institute for Eco-development and Cross Cultural Management (the EC^{2}M Institute). When analysing an investment it takes into account the classical anticipated cash flow, which leads to the much used IRR (internal rate of return) calculation as well as the anticipated costs needed so that the projected investment be environmentally neutral. Although the extra costs actually exist, they are mostly "hidden" from the economic equation and treated as externalities (cf Stern review). However, we propose to integrate them, especially the decommission costs and to calculate theintegrative internal rate of return (IIRR):

$$\sum_{i=1}^{N} \frac{CF_i - EcoCost_i}{(1 + r)^i}$$

where
CF	= cash flow of the project during its whole life cycle
EcoCost	= costs that are to be integrated which relate to the eco-impact
R	= rate of return
N	= number of periods (normally years).

On the proposed example the impact of the full picture can be easily appreciated (Figure 9.1).

Where an apparently high return (IRR) project becomes more realistic when all real cots are reintegrated, specifically those eco-costs which are treated as "externalities" today – basically meaning that somebody

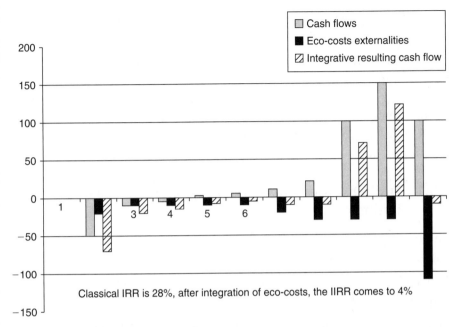

Figure 9.1 Integrative internal rate of return.

else external to the project picks up the costs which, at the moment, is the society (health cost burden for sweatshop workers), the tax payer (such as eco-labels on French vehicles), future generations (chemicals in soils and in underground water reserves), other nations (international supply chain, deforestation of rain forest, decimated biodiversity), etc.

9.5 How to control: from today's best concepts issuing from the UN and related think-tanks to real business world best practices

It is clear for most if not all scientists that we are currently at a turning point of history. However, it is less clear as to whether the only way out is via sustainable retreat or by sustainable growth. The latter hypothesis has been retained as the "official" scenario by the UN, OECD, EU and related governments bodies. In this respect, i.e., how corporations should behave with regard to sustainable growth, a set of international "soft laws" or international declarations and resolutions have been elaborated by the UN, OECD or the EU states during the past 10 years. This set of "soft laws" is being incorporated into directives issued by international organisations and professional bodies with corporate social responsibility (CSR).

Here again at this level, controlling for sustainability comes into play. Even if controlling for sustainability does not come first today, it will not be long before it takes a prominent place in the controlling function. Among the many initiatives, currently flourishing in this direction, five seem to be particularly geared with core controlling functions and are mentioned here.

9.5.1 Triple Bottom Line Reporting/Global Reporting Initiative

The concept here is to look at the impact of a corporation under three angles taken at the same level of importance (Figure 9.2):

The social performance, i.e., the way to treat employees, communities, extended suppliers, etc.

The environmental performance i.e., assessing what is the performance of the firm vis à vis the environment (effluents, emissions, pollutions, waste, etc.).

The economic/financial performance, which is what controllers only mainly focused on today.

The Triple Bottom Line reporting, otherwise known as Global Reporting Initiative (GRI), is a voluntary initiative fostered by the Geneva-based

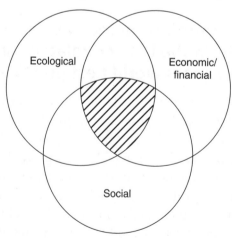

Figure 9.2 Triple bottom line reporting.

international NGO – the World Business Council for Sustainable Development (WBCSD). The WBCSD was actually founded by the Swiss industrialist and philanthropist, Stephan Schmidheiny, who was the driving force along with the UN secretary behind the first global environment summit in 1992: The "Rio Summit".

The Triple Bottom Line Reporting is performed by over 200 corporations worldwide, following a rigorous process. Regular updates are delivered by the GRI, and supported by UNEP. The most difficult part of this process is to define and consistently apply performance indicators for each of the three dimensions coupled with the extra difficulty in social and environmental reporting for which there is not enough literature nor accumulated experience as of yet on which to draw. Fortunately, a very promising avenue is the concept of "full life cycle assessment", and subsequently the eco-design, where a product, project or service impact on the environment is assessed to its full extent, and also from "cradle to grave" meaning from inception to decommissioning and to either re-use, re-cycle, or scrap.

Mini case: Where a Hybrid car can deliver a hybrid impact

Recently, a major US car eco-assessment found that although hybrid car's CO_2 emissions were lower than petrol vehicles due to the use of electric energy in combination with petrol, they were in fact not so "clean" when assessed on a full life basis because of the amount of pollution created upstream to manufacture the batteries and downstream at the end of their life when decommissioning the batteries.

Mini case: Hydroelectricity

The same conclusion was reached when a full life assessment was made on the impacts of hydroelectricity power generation when the severe damage caused to fauna and flora by the flooding of otherwise useful and bio-diverse lands is taken into the equation, e.g., the three river dams in China.

9.5.2 The Global Compact

Launched in 2000, this is a UN-led initiative that invites private, public sector operators and NGOs, on a voluntary basis, to adopt and report on a set of charters that cover:

Human rights
Labour standards
Environment
Anti-corruption.

The reporting is compatible with the above-mentioned GRI. Here again it can be seen that the role and function of the international controller is extended well beyond the purely classical economic role.

9.5.3 ISO

In the wake of its very famous 9000 Standard series dealing with "quality" and "quality management" the International Standardisation Organisation has recently launched a series of new standards, the 14 000 series dealing with "environment and environment management".

Among the interesting elements that constitute the ISO approach to environment, a concept developed in cooperation with UNEP of "full product life cycle" that can be singled out is where a product is analysed along its entire life including the disposal costs. This is particularly interesting for controllers. It is furthermore expected that in 2008 the ISO will release a series of standards dealing with corporate governance, the 27 000 series. As far as the controlling function is concerned, the interesting point here again is to acknowledge the expansion of the controller's role way beyond the financial role that used to be the core role of controllers until recently due to the new compliance to standards and the subsequent obligation of monitoring and reporting.

9.5.4 Banks: The World Bank Performance Standards

The World Bank and the International Finance Corporation (IFC), the private arm of the World Bank, have recently developed a series of performance indicators coupled with impact assessment related to environment and CSR as conditions sine qua non that must be fulfilled to grant a loan. It basically means that along with economic and financial performance indicators, environment and CSR indicators are deemed to be spelt out, identified, qualified, quantified and controlled. And controlled ex ante, as part of the investment dossier is a prior condition to be met to obtain the loan. As well as controlled ex post, as part of the mandatory monitoring, auditing and reporting process whilst the financed project is being unfold. The sustainability reporting is therefore put at the very core of the project's development by this very stringent condition.

9.5.5 Banks: the Equator Principles

Similarly for any project financing, a set of leading private banks have conditioned their loans to comply with very strict principles with regard to sustained growth, environment protection, communities respect, diversity respects, CSR, impact assessment, etc. Again all these parameters are to be identified and reported; thus falling within the scope of international and cross-cultural controlling.

9.5.6 Green Accounting: GDP a misleading indicator?

Many initiatives come under this wording. Even the United Nations Environment Programme (UNEP) has developed some guidance on this subject. Most the time the concept is another indicator that better reflect wellness and sustainability and acts as a substitute to the universally used GDP which measures economic growth.

Indeed GDP has many drawbacks.

Amongst the most widely voiced concerned criticism is that contrary to corporate accounting, GDP does not provide for depreciation nor amortisation, e.g., when oil is extracted to serve as fuel it is booked as an increase of the GDP at all stages of its sales, but there is no depreciation charge that would provide for the re-constitution of an equivalent resource. In accounting terms, it would be as if one would only count the sales in the P&L and forget to charge for the cost of the material sold and more specifically for the depreciation of the plant, machinery and equipment. This would simply violate the "continuity" principle which is mandatory in accounting to follow any kind of GAAPs. GDP does not recognise "home" work, i.e., non-merchant "green" economies like those found in abundance in developing countries. These are just not counted, e.g., subsistence farming is simply not part of GDP. GDP is, de facto, rewarding destruction and waste. For example, when a major complex of office buildings, commercial shopping centres and residence are built in a country, it increases the GDP; and when it realises for some reasons that building these was a mistake, it is then destroyed – the demolition work actually increases the GDP, and if finally a new equivalent complex is built few years later to replace the initial complex somewhereelse it increases the GDP again for the third time. Despite these flaws, GDP remains the leading economic indicator, although new indicators are being developed. For example a very interesting one is the Human Development Index, a composite indicator which, under the initiative of the UN and inspired by the Economics Nobel Prize winner Amartya Sen, incorporates other factors such as life expectancy, and literacy rate into the calculations.

9.5.7 De-carbonized accounting

Amongst the many issues posed by sustainability, and thus by controlling for sustainability, is the one that revolves around global warming. Global warming is no longer a hypothesis, it is now a scientific fact as recently confirmed by the IPCC under the auspices of the UN in November 2007. One the major "drivers" identified as causing climate change is the increasing level of greenhouse gases (GHG) being released into the atmosphere, of which carbon dioxide is accounted for causing most of the problem. The lesser the CO_2 in the air, the lesser the warming, thus the better the chances for a sustained development to occur. In brief, the buzzword is a de-carbonized economy or carbon-neutral business.

Why and how to control CO_2 emissions?
Firstly, an incentive scheme has been put in place particularly in the EU and in several regions to help move from theory to practice to make every player, starting with the major GHG emitters (industries) contribute to the EU formal goals which are to achieve a CO_2 emission reduction in the future as per the Kyoto Protocol. It must be noted that the United States, a major world CO_2 emitter, has still not ratified the Kyoto Protocol. In practice, the EU launched the ETS (European Emission Trading System) known as Carbon Emissions trading. A sort of stock

exchange was created where emissions would be allocated to member states in relation to the emissions of their most polluting industries as a sort of minimal "license to pollute". Those companies who have an allocation but exceed their quota are allowed to buy non-used credits from other European companies, thus creating a virtuous spiral rewarding the lower carbon emitter. In practice, the ETS encountered some difficulties relative to the over ex ante evaluation of member states' emission levels, and the "inventory" of credits was initially too high to create a minimum tension necessary for the offer and demand torque to work (nobody had anything to buy but only to sell). Briefly, the CO_2 ETS prices fell.

Summary

The world is at an important turning point, its environment is being destroyed by man-made industrial activities at incredibly fast pace. The main reason that this has gone undetected and uncontrolled until recently is that environmental destruction associated costs were treated as externalities to the economic equation as brilliantly stated by Nicholas Stern. Industrial activities have to now engage in a major turnaround to control the situation, and achieve sustainable growth, if that is still possible as hypothesised by the UN, EU, OECD and governments. However, this is challenged by many scientists like Lovelock, Meadows, Georgescu who advocate that it is too late and that the only way out is the sustainable retreat.

Controlling will be at the centre of the environment monitoring function within companies exactly as controllers were at the beginning of the industrialisation process one and half centuries ago. During that period, controllers invented tools and methods to keep industry and society abreast of the challenges, always developing more adequate, sophisticated and integrative costs models, accounting techniques, controls and monitoring mechanisms.

To integrate the environment is an even bigger challenge that controllers face today, not as a consideration aside, but as a full-fledged central factor to control. Already some interesting practical initiatives have been launched, such as the GRI, the ISO norms, or more conceptual ones such as the Stern Review or from the EC^{2}M Institute which provide models to factor-in the economic argument.

Unfortunately, there is the quasi-absence of structured research and core curriculum teachings in these fields in management, business and engineering schools, although it is precisely from these graduate schools that the minds and the business and scientific culture of the future managers, scientists and engineers are formed. Today only some scarce structured initiatives exist, such as the ones at Cambridge University in the United Kingdom in connection with the Prince of Wales initiative, or the Woods Institute at Standford University in the United States, or the joint ESCP–EAP European School of Management, École Centrale graduate school of Science and Engineering as well as the Institut d'Agronomie (Agronomics Institute) in France.

References

Allais, M. (1999), *La mondialisation, la destruction des emplois et de la croissance.*

Darwin, C.h. (1859), *The Origins of the Species.*

Georgescu-Roentgen, N. (1971), *The Entropy Law and the Economic Process.*

Gore, A. (2006), *An Inconvenient Truth.*

Lovelock, J. (1970), *Gaia Theory.*

Lovelock, J. (2006), *The Revenge of Gaia.*

Malthus, T. (1798), *An Essay on the Principle of Population.*

Marx, K. (1867), *Das Kapital.*

Meadows, et al. (1972), *Limits to Growth.*

Sen, A. (1999), *Development as Freedom.*

Stiglitz, J. (2002), *Globalisation and Its Discontents in 2002.*

UN (1983), *Our Common Future*, UN General Assembly resolution 38/161, 19 December.

UNESCO (2001), *Universal Declaration on Cultural Diversity.*

Conclusion

This book has taken you through a journey that brings together many facets of an international business's controlling and monitoring functions. Not only have the key levers of today been identified, but also those that will be prevailing in the future with respect to the 21st century challenges. International and cross-cultural winning typologies and models that promote long-term success from its engineering to its controlling have also been identified.

Beyond the technical tools and technology that may well look uniform, it has been seen that the international business models are diverse, because the world and the way business is done in different parts of the world is diverse.

Markets are not machines buying from machines, but people buying from people, and people are diverse and complex with "soft" factors such as cultures and values driving them. Diversity is an invariant constant of humankind.

Convergence and uniformity is a just a fallacy that provides the easy conceptual excuse to promote and "sell" a "one best way"; it is at most a political and ideological Trojan horse. It has also been seen that, from an economic point of view, those businesses which fail to address market and cultural diversity in an adequate and balanced way, with respect to their own cultures in the course of their internationalisation process, fail to deliver in the long term. Ultimately they disappear. Extinction rhymes with uniformisation.

Diversity in nations and cultures is not a problem to flatten nor an obstacle to explode. It is a unique opportunity from which to leverage and benefit, whereas if controlled and monitored *adequately* it works for the organisation, not against it.

Many authors have discussed cultural diversity: most of the time in a discursive sociological and anthropological way, sometimes with a linguistic and communication approach *but none has so far addressed the way to manage the cultures in relation to the enduring and sustainable international performance of an organisation in a comprehensive manner.*

This book achieves that.

Particularly, the author of this book, in a very innovative way, based on 4 years of the highest level of academic research coupled with 30 years of international and cross-cultural experience as an executive in and advisor to leading MNCs and international organisations in the world, provides both the breakthrough conceptual model and the metrics to do so.

The N12 MODEL coupled with the I^2Q diagnosis, prognosis and controlling system provides a unique and valuable support in the quest of enduring top international performance. It addresses the root drivers of the enduring top performance whilst identifying why some MNCs remain the best performers over hundreds of years or more, when others in the same market segments, with equivalent technology and capital, fail to deliver and ultimately disappear either by being absorbed or just going bankrupt.

Exactly in the same way as diversity in cultures is an ingredient of success, whilst not weeding it to eradicate it but seed it to nurture it, biodiversity preservation is essential to humankind's continuation.

Similar to cultures and values that have been so often excluded, economic calculations have forever left the environmental/eco-efficiency dimensions out of the equation since they were also always treated as "externalities".

Ways forward, such as the IIRR or others, coming from diverse think-tanks such as the Global Institute for Eco-Development and Cross-Cultural Management (EC^{2}M Institute) and from international organisations like the UN, EU, OECD, etc. have been explored to provide the controlling function with both the conceptual models and the hands on tools to help monitor this essential eco-dimension.

Despite this, business controlling and monitoring in an international context still cannot be addressed without reference to international *corporate governance*.

And here again, diversity is the invariant where again words used in different languages concerning the board members exemplify the situation perfectly:

In English, *director* conveys the sense of direction: the way forward, the strategy and guidance as well as the orders and the sense of command that cascade down the organisation. This organisation is led for action, to be decisive from the board of directors whereas theoretically it is one level below in executing the strategy, i.e., the executive board led by the CEO.

In German, the word for director is *Mitglied* der Verwaltungsrat. The important word here is Mitglied. Mit means "together" (or actually "with" in English) and "glied" means a member as a part. Therefore, the concept of collectivity comes first and takes precedence on even the individual's role. It is understood that things are firstly done collectively at the board level; then comes what has to be done together. Mitbestimmung is a corollary of mitglied. Mit (together) is again the key word and "bestimmung" is another key word: it means the decision-making process towards a destiny. Thus, literally what comes first in a German board of directors is to work *together towards deciding our joint future.*

In Spanish, the word for director is *Consejero/a*; literally this means "adviser". (Aconsejar: to advise). The concept conveyed here is a political conception of the corporation. Advisors are here to advise – the chief who ultimately makes the decisions, such as a king or a CEO.

In French, the word for director is *Administrateur*. It literally means the one who expedites the administration work. The French board of directors call themselves bureaucrats. The bureaucracy (another French originating word – a bureau means desk in French) is the primary factor, therefore, in a French board of directors' formation. This is a typical French cultural trait. It also reads that the French board does not define the strategy per se, the CEO does it in practice, regardless of the concept that may be introduced to optically comply with some legal requirement.

In Asia, the board of director is often just notional: most of the time the real shareholders do not even appear in the records, which does not mean that they are not known to the stakeholders and management.

Like corporate governance the controlling and monitoring functions are both at the crux of the matter for the business community to successfully adjust to the ever-growing internationalisation and all its ramifications. For example, recently, a major French bank (Société Générale) posted an all-time record in "evaporating" no less than 7 billion euros in uncontrolled and unmonitored international speculations with its clients' money. It is more than seven times the amount that provoked the Barings Bank collapse in 1995. And the irony is that the chairman of the board of this bank (Société Générale) chartered by the French government in 2002 to come up with a white book on corporate governance to moralise business practices in the wake of the Enron, WorldCom and Arthur Andersen scandals. His white book stressed on auditing and controlling, and has been embedded into a new business law that now prevails in France (e.g., the combined code in the UK or Sarbanes–Oxley in the United States).

Thus, the real challenge is in the capacity to enact, control and monitor the ensuing changes with sufficient vigour and in an adequate time frame for all stakeholders to continue living in harmony. I hope this book, by exploring many promising new avenues, has given you the appetite to apply them in your international businesses.

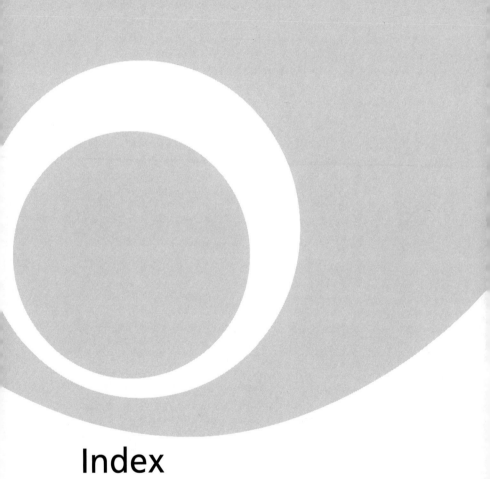

Index

4796 224